The Hydroponic Hot House

Low-Cost, High-Yield Greenhouse Gardening

James B. DeKorne

Loompanics Unlimited
Port Townsend, Washington

This book is sold for information purposes only. Neither the author nor the publisher will be held accountable for the use or misuse of the information contained in this book.

Some of the information in this book has been compiled and updated from articles originally written by the author in various issues of *The Mother Earth News*, and in two chapters in *The Solar Greenhouse Book*, Rodale Press, 1978.

Published by:
Loompanics Unlimited
P.O. Box 1197
Port Townsend, WA 98368
Loompanics Unlimited is a division of Loompanics Enterprises, Inc.

Front cover photo by James B. DeKorne. Back cover photo by John McKelvey. Unless otherwise noted, all photos courtesy of James B. DeKorne.

Illustrations by Barbara Williams

ISBN 1-55950-079-4
Library of Congress Catalog Card Number 91-Pending

Contents

1

Author's Confession
and Introduction

Prediction is very difficult, especially about the future.
— Niels Bohr

This book, ***The Hydroponic Hot House***, is a completely revised and updated rendition of *The Survival Greenhouse*, which was first published in 1975 by the Walden Foundation. A second edition was printed by Peace Press in 1978 — it differed from the initial version only by the addition of a Table of Contents and Index. The volume in your hands has been significantly changed from the first two.

The original book did quite well, considering its counter-culture origins and the fact that the only advertising consisted of some favorable reviews in the alternative press. I suspect that the title had something to do with its success: the word "Survival" has connotations which evoke an anxiety in many of us that the established world order is not stable enough to rely upon for our basic sustenance.

The concepts behind the original book were conceived, researched and written up in a climate of anxious expectation that "civilization as we know it" was about to disintegrate. The consequences of the Vietnam war, Watergate and the Arab Oil Embargo, plus increasing economic instability and a terrible sense of impending ecological disaster all seemed to be converging somewhere just over the horizon. One did not have to look too far in those days to find some version of a doomsday "scenario" predicting utter catastrophe within only a few years.

The famous Club of Rome report, *The Limits to Growth* (1972), had a great deal of influence on many people's thinking, including my own. The three conclusions outlined in the introduction to that book were a compelling demand for action — or so it seemed at the time. Here's the first one:

> 1. If the present growth trends in world population, industrialization, pollution, food production, and resource depletion continue unchanged, the limits to growth on this planet will be reached sometime within the next one hundred years. The most probable result will be a rather sudden and uncontrollable decline in both population and industrial capacity.

The dry understatement of the last sentence only served to inflame my imagination as to what might be expected when this "probable result" came about, particularly when augmented by less conservatively worded images, such as this one from Dr. Paul Ehrlich:

Most of the people who are going to die in the greatest cataclysm in the history of man have already been born. More than three and a half billion people already populate our moribund globe, and about half of them are hungry. Some 10 to 20 million will starve to death *this year*... (By 1975) some experts feel that food shortages will have escalated the present level of world hunger and starvation into famines of unbelievable proportions. Other experts, more optimistic, think the ultimate food-population collision will not occur until the decade of the 1980's.

— Paul Ehrlich, "Eco-Catastrophe!," *Ramparts*, Sept., 1969

If *this* was what was waiting for us over the near horizon, then obviously it was time for concerned citizens to do something about it. Perhaps things weren't totally hopeless. The Club of Rome's second conclusion optimistically suggested that a kind of utopia was even attainable:

2. It is possible to alter these growth trends and to establish a condition of ecological and economic stability that is sustainable far into the future. The state of global equilibrium could be designed so that the basic material needs of each person on earth are satisfied and each person has an equal opportunity to realize his individual human potential.

For a utopian like myself, weaned on Sixties activism and imbued with the idealist philosophies of Emerson and Thoreau, such an agenda was a marvelous new challenge. Certainly *The Limits to Growth* left no doubt about the urgent need for some kind of immediate action in its third and final conclusion:

3. If the world's people decide to strive for this second outcome rather than the first, the sooner they begin working to attain it, the greater will be their chances of success.

So in the best traditions of liberal, world-saving optimism coupled with Thoreauvian self-reliance, I began working on it

— and eventually evolved the idea of a self-sustaining greenhouse, a mini "eco-system" that could be used by anyone seeking a measure of self-sufficiency and freedom from the (as I wrote in the introduction to the first edition) "corporate whims of the marketplace." I hasten to add that I make no claims for having "invented" any of these concepts — they were in the air in those days, and many individuals and groups were developing their own versions of them. The New Alchemy Institute, for example, was working along the same lines, and I was greatly influenced by their ideas — particularly in the field of aquaculture.

In looking through old notebooks while revising this book I found a mimeographed hand-out dating from the mid-seventies. It serves as well as anything to reveal my original beliefs, mindset, and the concepts that evolved out of them. I beg the reader's indulgence with my "facts:"

A Brief Description of the Eco-System Greenhouse
Three Facts:

1. Modern agriculture has become totally dependent upon a rapidly dwindling supply of fossil fuels at a time that mankind is experiencing the first stages of a world-wide famine.

2. Exacerbated by an extremely unstable energy and economic situation, the effects of this famine will soon begin to be felt in the United States.

3. Since they do not raise it themselves, few people have any control whatsoever over the source of their food. Neither have they much control over the money they need to purchase this food.

These conditions suggest that those people who can grow most or all of their own sustenance will be the ones best able to care for themselves during the times ahead. The eco-system greenhouse was designed to do this by meeting the following criteria:

1. The eco-system greenhouse is designed to provide a maximum amount of food within the framework of an ecologically sound technology. No non-renewable sources of energy are used.

2. The eco-system greenhouse is designed to be within the economic reach of even the poorest families. Once the basic concepts are mastered, it can be operated by anyone.

3. Once in full operation, the eco-system greenhouse should be capable of meeting most of the food requirements of a small family.

To maximize its yields, the eco-system greenhouse makes use of the following techniques:

1. *Hydroponic Gardening.* The hydroponic method alone will triple the yield of produce over conventional methods from an equivalent area of growing space. An organically derived hydroponic solution is now being researched which will enable the individual to make his own. Rabbit manure and earthworm castings are the primary source for this.

2. *Carbon Dioxide.* The addition of CO_2 to a greenhouse atmosphere can increase crop yields up to seventy percent. We keep four adult rabbits (three does, one buck) in the greenhouse, each one of which produces about 40 grams of CO_2 per day through the normal process of respiration.

3. *Maximized Rabbit Production.* A female rabbit will normally produce four litters a year: an annual average of 84 offspring for the three females. Harvested when they attain a weight of five pounds, the total is 420 pounds of protein per year, or 105 pounds of meat per person per year for a family of four.

4. *Aquaculture.* Statistics vary for different conditions, but intensive aquaculture, or fish farming, can produce a significantly large proportion of protein each year. We are presently experimenting with various techniques to maximize production in this sphere.

The core motivations behind my exploration were to gain maximum food output from a minimum energy input and drain on the environment. Although the entropy law states that there can be no gain without some loss, the challenge was to reduce that loss as much as reasonably possible. While it is true that there aren't any free lunches in this world, it seemed to me that some lunches could be made considerably cheaper than others. When you reflect on the statistic that agribusiness practices in the United States in the seventies required an input of about *twenty* calories of energy in the form of petroleum to produce only *one* calorie of energy in the form of food, it's obvious that we'd be further ahead if we could learn to drink gasoline! I don't know if this twenty-to-one caloric ratio is still valid for the nineties, but I suspect that it hasn't changed too much.

The metaphor within which I sought my alternatives was that of the eco-system. The dictionary defines an eco-system as "an ecological community considered together with the non-living factors of its environment as a unit." The key here is the phrase: "as a unit" — an eco-system isn't so much a *thing* as it is a holistic *process*; as such, it is also a world-view, a way of perceiving life.

The original book was a description of my experimentation with the eco-system concept as applied to intensive food production in a closed system. In essence, I was trying to duplicate (and control) a complete process of nature within the confines of a highly artificial man-made environment.

Perhaps I may be forgiven such naive hubris — after all, my intentions were good. I no longer believe that it is useful (or even possible) to do this. Real eco-systems are so complex that even ecologists don't claim to understand them completely. Although the ideal of maintaining an ecological balance of forces in any greenhouse is certainly worth striving for, the grower should allow herself a little slack in how she brings it about. The concept of ecology refers to the real world undergoing change, and humans and their artifacts must be included in the process.

Since all eco-systems are local, any greenhouse is going to respond to the environment in which it exists. My environment is a fairly harsh one. A desert is defined as an area with less than ten inches of annual rainfall, and semi-arid environments receive between ten and twenty inches. My village in New Mexico, at an elevation of 7,000 feet above sea level, receives a yearly average of 11.76 inches of precipitation.

Although this is a dry climate, it isn't a particularly hot one; because of the high altitude, the annual mean temperature is about 47 degrees F., and it is only during June, July and August that the monthly mean temperature rises above 60 degrees. Thus in an area that receives barely 1.7 inches more rainfall than an official desert, we only have a 90 day (sometimes more, sometimes less) growing season. The latest and earliest frosts I can remember came on June 8th and August 28th respectively.

Even hard-scrabble subsistence agriculture is difficult here. In the old days, the local economy revolved around sheep and cattle ranching, though in recent years this has become increasingly marginal due to overgrazing. These environmental conditions are generally typical of the Hispanic villages in Northern New Mexico, and explain why the area has until the last ten years at least, remained relatively unspoiled by development.

Needless to say, it is extremely difficult to raise even a subsistence crop under such circumstances, and it was because of this that I began casting about for alternatives. The main questions were: How could I extend the growing season, overcome the extreme scarcity of water, attain maximum yields with minimum waste, yet still retain reasonable ease of operation? The only restriction I placed on this search was that the solutions had to be consistent with ecological reality — only natural, non-polluting systems would be considered.

The prototype unit, an underground greenhouse and aquaculture tank (see Figure 1-1), was described in Volume #28 of *The Mother Earth News* as follows:

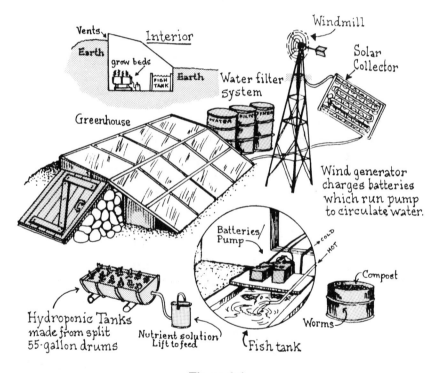

Figure 1-1

The original concept for the eco-system greenhouse incorporated alternative energy source, hydroponics and aquaculture.

This is the first article in a series describing the construction and use of a complete "eco-system" — an underground hydroponic greenhouse and aquaculture tank: powered by the wind, heated by the sun and fed on compost.

The unit, built on our small homestead in Northern New Mexico (altitude: 7,000 feet), is still in the experimental stages, but preliminary results have far surpassed our expectations... The greenhouse — four feet below ground level and banked with earth on the north side — utilizes a 1,400 gallon solar-heated fish tank as a heat source for winter vegetable growing. A 12-volt, 200-watt Wincharger supplies the power to circulate the water through filters and a small flat-plate solar heat collector. The liquid in the fish tank acts as a "heat battery," collecting solar energy during the daytime and radiating it back into the greenhouse at night.

The vegetables are grown hydroponically in 55-gallon drums cut in half lengthwise and filled with gravel. Under the eight hydroponic tanks are two additional drums cut in half horizontally to make four compost bins in which earthworms are raised. The worms are used to feed the fish, and the worm castings are leached to make the organic hydroponic solution which feeds the plants.

Our eco-system was designed to be almost completely self-sustaining. The wind generates the electricity which runs the water-circulating pump, the sun heats the water and the heated (and filtered) liquid keeps the fish happy and warms the greenhouse at night. The worms and their byproducts provide food for fish and plants. The only substance that comes in from 'outside' is the organic matter which feeds the worms, and that from no farther away than our animal pens and compost heap...

In theory, at least, this is the description of a self-sustaining eco-system: a basic food-producing unit capable of supplementing the diet of a small family. If it is true that hydroponic methods hold the potential of more than tripling the harvest of agricultural crops, and if organic aquaculture can produce similar yields of aquatic protein, then it should be possible for any family or small community to produce a large portion of its nutritional requirements from a very small area of ground, in almost any environment. (See Figure 1-2)

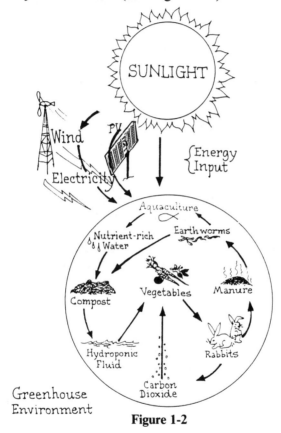

Figure 1-2

Mandala for a greenhouse eco-system, showing the ideal interaction of forces.

As we shall see, the process isn't quite as simple as my original enthusiasm would have made it. The "present tense" style in which *The Mother Earth News* article was written is rather misleading, reflecting a naive optimism common to writing of this type during the seventies. Much of the stuff appearing in the back-to-the-land publications from that era converted unproven hypotheses into established facts. I am not proud to admit that I am responsible for my own share of it. The fact is that a lot of blue-sky experiments-in-progress were presented as established facts, not because we were liars, but because we were so earnestly convinced of their favorable outcome.

This publication is a description of my on-going experience with those original concepts and an attempt to put them into some realistic perspective.

First of all, one often hears the claim that a greenhouse of less than 200 square feet is capable of feeding a family of four. Such statements are misleading. With skill and proper management, greenhouses between 150 and 250 square feet are capable of supplying a large part of a family's diet, but not, by any means I know of, capable of providing *all* of it. Thus the word "Survival" in the original title of this book was probably too ambitious in its connotations.

With that off my chest, let me go on to state that a small greenhouse of the type described in these pages will, if properly managed, surely enhance the quality of your life. Whether or not you will be able to "survive" because of it I have no way of knowing — it will certainly provide you with a lot of fresh produce for at least eight months of the year.

You won't find here a blueprint for the construction of a 100-percent efficient free lunch machine, but instead the description of a continuing experiment, including some educated opinions on how it might be improved. The attentive reader will find many changes, additions, omissions and revisions in this edition.

For example, the Attached Greenhouse is now my preferred design, being in most ways superior to the pit greenhouse originally described. In addition, wind electric systems are now all but obsolete (except at very specialized locations), having been replaced by photovoltaic panels. I even now question the necessity of having such systems as a source of power for a greenhouse.

In the plus column, in my opinion, the chapter on hydroponics, updated to include the Nutrient Flow Technique (NFT), is alone worth the price of this book. The method comes the closest of anything I've seen yet to equaling the extravagant claims made for it. (Indeed, it almost constitutes a "free lunch!")

Aquaculture, alas, remains problematic. Of all of the new concepts which were hyped during the seventies, greenhouse aquaculture is probably the one which has had the most disappointing results. I have not yet given up on aquaculture, however, and, at the end of that chapter, I outline one idea which I think holds promise.

It must also be noted that, while the general features of the eco-system should be applicable almost anywhere, specific changes for environments drastically different from mine would be required. Obviously, my greenhouse was designed to function in response to the characteristics of the larger eco-system which surrounds it. High altitude, plus low temperatures and precipitation were but a few of the factors which had to be regarded. Each area has its own natural characteristics which must be taken into consideration.

Having given the reader these caveats, let me conclude this first chapter by saying unequivocally that the construction of a home greenhouse, whether or not you intend to manage it as a pure "eco-system," is well worth the trouble and expense, and will repay your efforts many times over. You will find in this book many useful ideas for maximizing the production from any greenhouse.

2

Greenhouse Basics

Most plant life goes quiescent below 50 degrees, and this means that although plants may stay in the sunpit (green-house) without freezing, they will neither grow nor open their flowers until the February sun sends the temperature inside soaring.

— Fred Lape, *Organic Gardening,* February, 1977

The different components of the eco-system are so interrelated that it is difficult to know where to start. Since the process is a continuous cycle of relationships, any given starting point is the "middle." However, since the greenhouse itself provides the environment within which our eco-system functions, that is where we shall begin.

Forcing Structures

Most of the literature refers to the greenhouse as a "forcing structure" — an artificial environment where plants can be "forced" to grow, even though the conditions outside the structure may be hostile to plant survival. Since two of the many factors necessary for plant life are heat and light, it follows that the minimum requirements of any forcing structure will be to retain warmth and allow light to enter, thus providing a mini-environment favorable to plant growth.

The greenhouse, then, is designed in response to the light and temperature fluctuations in the yearly cycle of the seasons; if we all lived on the equator, with its year-round growing season, forcing structures would be unnecessary. The use of a forcing structure enables a gardner to increase the growing season from several weeks to several months, depending upon where he lives and the type of forcing structure he uses.

Like any use of "force" however, there is a point of diminishing returns in how far it can be implemented. For greenhouse gardeners in most northern temperate climates, the point of diminishing returns usually arrives sometime in the mid-autumn. The reasons for this are straightforward enough, though they are unfortunately not yet commonly understood: among those who haven't actually tried it, the myth of year-round greenhouse gardening continues to be a popular fantasy.

The Zodiacal Calendar

We know that in the Northern Hemisphere the sun is at its zenith on the summer solstice — June 21st, and at its nadir on the winter solstice — December 21st — respectively, the longest and shortest days in the year. The midpoints, when the days and nights are of equal length, are the equinoxes — March 21st and September 21st. Each one of these four days in the year marks the beginning of a season — summer and winter on the solstices, spring and autumn on the equinoxes.

Modern urbanites have become estranged from the significance of these very important dates in the yearly cycle, though pre-industrial and ancient cultures built their religious holidays around them. For example, in pre-Christian Rome, December 25th, our Christmas, marked the Saturnalia, a winter solstice celebration.

Effective Growing Season

In working with the natural forces of the eco-system, I soon observed that the growing year really did seem to organize itself around the dates of the zodiacal calendar. If you can imagine each of the zodiacal months as one hour in a twelve-hour day, then dawn is the spring equinox, dusk is the autumnal equinox and noon and midnight are the solstices. Plant growth noticeably begins to fall off around the 21st of October — an "hour after sunset" in the yearly day, and it isn't until about the 21st of February, "one hour before dawn," that plant growth again seems to prosper. This provides an *effective growing season* of roughly eight months. I wish to emphasis that I am not qualified to make any claims for or against astrology — I am merely using what, for the purposes of greenhouse gardening in this area, is an accurate and convenient frame of reference to describe the yearly indoor growth cycle. (See Figure 2-1.)

The concept of the *effective growing season* is one of the most important points made in this book, and it can hardly be over-emphasized: *Under ordinary circumstances, plant growth during deep winter in most sections of the United States, will not result in enough edible tissue to justify the effort or expense of cul-*

tivating it. You can keep your tomato plants *alive* over the winter period, and you may harvest a salad or two from your lettuce plants, but food-production levels during the period of October 21st to February 21st will probably be but a pitiful fraction of what you'll harvest during the rest of the year.

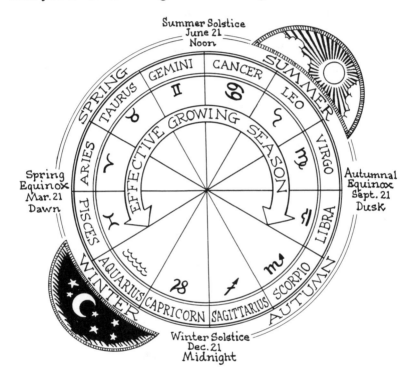

Figure 2-1

*The zodiacal calendar, showing the **effective growing season** for greenhouse gardening in most areas of the United States.*

It is an unfortunate fact that the tenacious myth of a twelve-month greenhouse growing season refuses to disappear. Here, for example, is a quote from the brochure of a commercial greenhouse manufacturer:

"...Overnight you are a 12-month-out-of-the-year gardener... The (Brand Name) Greenhouse gives you fresh strawberry shortcake in December, watermelon on New Year's Day and fresh, fresh vegetables year-round."

Unless these individuals know something that I don't, the kindest thing that I can say about the above statement is that it is highly misleading. Because it is so important, we shall return more than once to this subject of *effective growing season* in the pages that follow.

Photosynthesis

When we speak of plant growth, we are largely speaking of the process of photosynthesis — the miracle by which green plants are able to draw their essential energy and create living matter directly from sunlight. The *Encyclopedia Britannica* gives us a capsule definition:

Photosynthesis is the process by which higher plants manufacture dry matter through the aid of chlorophyll pigment, which uses solar energy to produce carbohydrates out of water and carbon dioxide. The overall efficiency of this critical process is somewhat low and its mechanics are extremely complex... *The amount of light, the carbon dioxide supply, and the temperature are the three most important environmental factors that directly affect the rate of photosynthesis*; water and minerals in sufficient quantities also are necessary. (Emphasis mine.)

Heat and Light

To provide an optimum space for photosynthesis to take place, greenhouses are designed to admit light and retain heat: If the *temperature* rises above or falls below certain limits, plant growth (photosynthesis) will cease. Similarly, if the *intensity* and *duration* of light do not meet certain minimum standards, growth is also checked. This latter factor is extremely important and seems not to be well understood by many people. The reason that the period from October 21st to February 21st produces minimal plant growth is because this is the time of the year in the Northern Hemisphere when the *intensity* and *duration* of light and heat are at their lowest levels. Maintaining adequate lighting in the winter greenhouse is a bit more complex than maintaining adequate temperature, so we will discuss it in a chapter all to itself. For now, we'll confine ourselves to the greenhouse as a temperature-efficient structure.

Greenhouse Types

There are generally five different types of forcing structures — the cold frame, the hot-bed, the free-standing greenhouse, the pit greenhouse, and the attached greenhouse.

The Cold Frame

The cold frame is typically a small box-like structure with a removable glass or plastic cover. It is usually used to protect seedlings in the early springtime, thus enabling a gardener to extend her growing season by several weeks. In effect, the cold frame is a very small, unheated greenhouse.

The Hot Bed

The hot bed, on the other hand, is a cold frame with an auxiliary heat source. In the old days, hot beds utilized fresh manure as a source of heat — warmth given off by the composting manure kept the plants from freezing. In more recent times, electric wires embedded in the soil of the hot bed accomplish the same purpose at a greater cost in energy.

The Free-standing Greenhouse

Figure 2-2

The free-standing greenhouse, while quite useful, is not compatible with the kind of alternative-energy gardening described in this book.

The word "greenhouse" itself conjures up the image, in most people's minds, of a free-standing, heated glass building used primarily for the propagation of flowers and other ornamental plants. Before the recent energy crisis, this stereotype was generally correct, for home greenhouses have historically been recreational structures — environments where plant enthusiasts raised exotic ornamentals for the envy and admiration of their garden clubs. It is significant to note that until the mid-seventies, at least, virtually every available book on greenhouse gardening was devoted almost exclusively to flower-culture. The literature which did deal with vegetable crops (usually tomatoes) was aimed at the huge commercial greenhouses which are usually run along agribusiness lines and were not (up until that time, anyway) typically concerned with energy conservation.

In general, conventional free-standing greenhouses, because they are difficult to insulate and hence have a greater need for auxiliary (usually fossil-fueled) heating sources, are not optimally suitable for the kind of growing strategies outlined in this book. That does not mean that they are not useful — I recently purchased an 8' x 15' free-standing fiberglass greenhouse that extends my growing season significantly, and gives me more space for the constantly proliferating plants in my life. All things being equal, however, pit and attached greenhouses are considerably more energy efficient than the freestanding types, and it is these latter designs which I will emphasize in these pages.

The Pit Greenhouse

Just as the hot bed is a variation on the simpler cold frame, the free-standing greenhouse is related in similar fashion to the older and more energy-efficient pit greenhouse. Ken Kern, in his book, *The Ownerbuilt Homestead* (1974), informs us that:

> The oldest reported forcing structure in the U.S. was not a greenhouse as we know it today. It was, rather, a pit covered with glass on the south side, and earth insulation on the north. This so-called pit greenhouse was built into the side of a Waltham, Massachusetts hill around 1800.

America's first greenhouse, then, was a pit greenhouse, designed to take advantage of the insulating properties of the earth — certainly a more energy-efficient structure than a glass framework exposed on all sides to the weather and requiring large inputs of heat to maintain its temperature during the spring, fall, and winter.

The rationale for a pit greenhouse is very simple: a few inches below the frost line, the earth maintains a constant year-round temperature of about 50 degrees F. If you put your greenhouse underground, you can take advantage of the insulating properties of the earth. It makes good sense: if the nighttime pit greenhouse temperature in early spring drops to 40 degrees F. (unless the face is unusually well-insulated, some of the previous day's gain will be lost through the glazing), it still only needs to gain 20 degrees to reach the 60 degrees optimum for cool-season crops. An uninsulated, unheated free-standing greenhouse would drop down to freezing or lower under the same circumstances, so the earth insulation of the pit greenhouse offers a definite advantage. (I am figuring an outside temperature of about 20 degrees F. — my unheated pit greenhouse consistently maintained nighttime temperatures at least 20 degrees warmer than those outside. Thus, if the outside thermometer dropped to 30 degrees F. at night, the greenhouse would normally stay at 50 degrees during the same period.)

Although pit greenhouses are still not very common, the concept of earth insulation for agricultural buildings has never really died out. Even America's first greenhouse is apparently still in operation. In Kathryn Taylor and Edith Gregg's book, *Winter Flowers in Greenhouse and Sun-heated Pit* (1969), a history of greenhouses is presented, along with photographs of the original Waltham, Massachusetts structure. Also described is the construction and use of their own simple pit greenhouse design. This structure is basically a pit dug into the ground with a peaked roof of glass built over it at a forty-five degree angle to take advantage of the low winter sun. Greenhouses of this type are often called "sunpits."

The Lama Grow-Hole

Figure 2-3

The "Lama Grow-Hole" shown here was an early inspiration for my own pit greenhouse.

My original introduction to pit greenhouses came from the Lama Foundation's "Grow-Hole" poster, mentioned on page 59 of *The Last Whole Earth Catalog* (1971). The structure was built around 1969 or 1970 at an altitude of 8,600 feet by the Lama Foundation on their land near Taos, New Mexico. It consisted of an excavation dug into a south-facing slope which was then shored up and framed with timber — making it resemble the vinyl-glazed entrance to some kind of exotic mine-shaft. (See Figure 2-3.)

Some time after reading the Grow-Hole Poster, I visited another pit greenhouse which had been made from the cellar hole of a burned-out ranch house. This gave me the idea that a Grow-Hole doesn't necessarily have to be built into a south-facing hillside. At that time I hadn't yet seen Taylor and Gregg's book, so was ignorant of their design.

In those days I was convinced that pit greenhouses were the only type that made any sense at all, and accordingly, in the spring of 1972, I hired a backhoe to dig a 12 by 24 foot hole in the field in front of my house. Because I was interested in pursuing aquaculture, a 1,400 gallon fish tank was incorporated into the design, and most of my early greenhouse experience was gained from the resulting structure. (See Figure 2-4.)

As fate would have it, this first greenhouse of mine was effectively ruined one night several years later when flooding irrigation water from a neighbor's field damaged it past the point of practical restoration. Fortunately, my interests had by then evolved far beyond that particular design and type of greenhouse, so the accident was not as devastating as it might have been a few years earlier.

Although each greenhouse type possesses specific advantages and disadvantages, I will focus most of my comments on the one

design most useful for homeowners. I have devoted the next
chapter to the so-called Attached Solar Greenhouse.

Figure 2-4

*Photograph of the author's original "Survival Greenhouse" as it
appeared upon completion circa 1973.*

3

The Attached
Solar Greenhouse

*Many of the systems I see are high on the Rube Goldberg
factor. I think the key to making an alternate energy system
work for you is to keep it as simple as possible. There are
a lot of complicated things you can do to make a greenhouse work better, but they all demand your time, energy,
and money. It's best to have a good design for your area
and work within its limitations.*

— Bill Yanda

An attached greenhouse is really nothing more than its name
implies — a thermally efficient forcing structure attached to the
south side of a dwelling with provision for venting the collected

heat into the house. It didn't take long for me to realize that the carefully collected solar energy being spilled from my pit greenhouse to the outdoors was being stupidly wasted. On many a winter day while I was stoking the parlor stove with firewood that I'd spent long hard hours in cutting and splitting, I was simultaneously dumping an equal amount of heat from the greenhouse to dissipate in the frigid outside air. Had the forcing structure been an integral part of my dwelling, I could have saved most of my wood, not to mention much of the labor that went into its collection and preparation. (See Figure 3-1.)

Figure 3-1

The author's home circa 1977, with newly attached greenhouse.

The principal advantage of an attached greenhouse, then, is not that it will grow more or better plants, but that it is an amazingly efficient heat collector for your dwelling. On a good sunny winter day it should heat all adjoining rooms and, assuming an efficient thermal storage system, that heat will be retained for most of the night. An accepted rule of thumb is that one square foot of greenhouse space will meet the requirements of between one and three square feet of dwelling space — as always, depending on conditions.

In a survey of attached greenhouse owners that I did back in the seventies I received overwhelmingly enthusiastic responses to questions concerning their heating efficiency. One architect-designed structure in Arizona receives about 80 percent of its winter heat from the greenhouse. Another homeowner stated that his greenhouse chopped $400.00 a year from his winter propane bill. That kind of performance suggests that this type of forcing structure will pay for itself in a very short time.

Most attached greenhouses consist of an ordinary stud framework which is built onto the south wall of a home, then double-glazed and insulated. The floors usually consist of masonry or flagstone to absorb and store heat. Water drums are also commonly used for this purpose. (See Chapter 4 for details on these principles.)

Many retrofits utilize the existing doors and windows in the house as ventilators, but depending upon the type of home and the construction ability of the builder, a more sophisticated venting system is possible. This begins with floor-level vents which admit cool air from the house into the greenhouse. As the lower-temperature inside air is heated, it naturally rises within the greenhouse to return through ceiling-level vents into your home. The convection current thus created essentially transforms the united structures into a kind of two-chambered heat engine. In this way, relatively cool air is always circulating from the house (bringing with it lots of essential carbon dioxide for the plants), being warmed in the greenhouse, and then vented back to the dwelling many degrees warmer than when it entered.

After sunset, the process can be reversed — the now cooler air from the greenhouse enters the home where it is warmed by your heating system, rises, and reenters the greenhouse. Due to the restrictions imposed by the effective growing season, however, many people prefer to close the vents at night, using the greenhouse primarily as a daytime heat collector during the winter rather than a place to raise any significant number of plants.

When building a new house with a greenhouse attached, it is useful to install the floor level vents from the dwelling against the far north wall of the interior room and utilize the space between the floor joists as a duct into the greenhouse. In this way the coldest air is always drawn from the room to be heated. The space between the joists, of course, must be sealed and insulated in such a way that only the inside room air enters the greenhouse — otherwise, cold air under the house will constantly enter the greenhouse, to no advantage at all!

During the summer, of course, the last thing you want to do is heat your dwelling, so the ventilators to the house must be kept closed. To keep the summer plants from cooking, an auxiliary venting system must be employed which circulates the heated greenhouse air outside. This may be accomplished by building a ground-level vent to admit cool outside air on the upwind side of the greenhouse, and a high vent to expel the hot greenhouse air on the downwind side. Such an orientation will ensure the efficient and continuous circulation of air. Some sort of windbreak in front of the low vent may be necessary in high wind areas, but since wind velocities are lowest in the Northern Hemisphere during the summer months when these vents are used most, high winds shouldn't be a problem. (See Figure 3-2.)

Bill Yanda, the man who did the most to pioneer the concept of attached greenhouses back in the seventies, states in his book, *The Food and Heat Producing Solar Greenhouse*:

> The total square footage of exterior vents should be about one-sixth of the floor area of the greenhouse. The high vent is one third larger than the lower one.

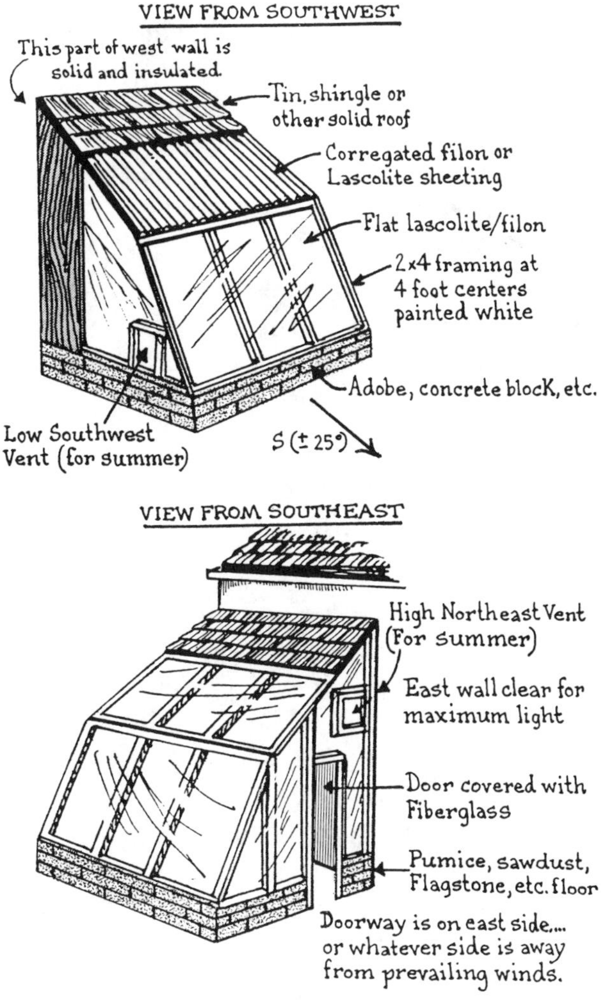

VIEW FROM SOUTHWEST

This part of west wall is solid and insulated.

Tin, shingle or other solid roof

Corregated filon or Lascolite sheeting

Flat lascolite/filon

2x4 framing at 4 foot centers painted white

Adobe, concrete block, etc.

Low Southwest Vent (for summer)

S (± 25°)

VIEW FROM SOUTHEAST

High Northeast Vent (For summer)

East wall clear for maximum light

Door covered with Fiberglass

Pumice, sawdust, Flagstone, etc. floor

Doorway is on east side.... or whatever side is away from prevailing winds.

Figure 3-2

Schematic drawing of a typical attached greenhouse.

Because of our arid New Mexico environment, I have never had humidity problems in my greenhouses. Obviously in parts of the country where the air-moisture content exceeds ours, high humidity can present serious difficulties in any greenhouse which vents into a dwelling. Adequate ventilation in summer is therefore a must, and in some climates might necessitate the use of an electric blower of some sort.

Despite all precautions, greenhouse humidity levels will reach the point where a safe wood preservative must be applied to all wooden surfaces to prevent rot. The recommended wood preservative for greenhouses is copper napthenate.

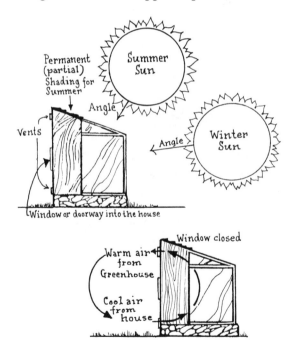

Figure 3-3

Schematic drawing of attached greenhouse, showing summer and winter sun angles and ventilation.

Essential to the design of any attached solar greenhouse is the incorporation of a partially glazed roof — one that allows the low winter sun to fully enter the structure, but will also block or shade most of the higher-angled summer radiation. (See Figure 3-3.) It is this simple but ingenious feature which prevents high temperatures from rendering the house unlivable in the summer, yet allows for a maximum amount of solar energy to enter in wintertime. One half to two thirds of the upper portion of the roof — the part that butts up against the house — should be opaque.

Another common rule of thumb is that for optimum efficiency an attached greenhouse should be about twice as long as it is wide. Be that as it may, I personally would never build an attached greenhouse less than eight feet or more than ten feet wide, no matter what the length was. Ten feet is a good width — it gives plenty of growing room while still remaining efficient as a solar collector.

So far, I have given all of the practical, common sense, dollars and cents reasons why I think an attached greenhouse is the best design for most homeowners. Perhaps the most compelling reason, however, is an aesthetic one: having a room full of plants attached to your living area will significantly enrich your everyday life. You will find yourself spending more and more time just being in the greenhouse — it will soon become the place to eat meals, entertain guests, take naps and just hang out. Of course, the more time you spend with your plants, the more you learn about their requirements and the healthier they (and you) become.

Access

The best book I know of about the design and construction of attached greenhouses is *The Food and Heat Producing Solar*

Greenhouse — Design, Construction, Operation, by Rick Fisher and Bill Yanda, John Muir Publications, P.O. Box 613, Santa Fe, NM 87501, 1976.

It is my understanding that this book is still in print.

4

Alternative Sources of Energy

Experience has shown that few wind machines can develop sufficient output at the low wind speeds (under 9 mph average) common in most locations. Even fewer have proven to be reliable over the long haul — not surprising when you consider that the thing must withstand a terrible beating from the weather. If wind is your only hope, look for a reconditioned Jacobs machine from the 30s through the 50s. They are virtually the only ones with a good rep. Under most conditions, PV is a better deal.

— J. Baldwin, *Whole Earth Ecolog*

To emphasize the last sentence above, I'll repeat it in italics: *Under most conditions, PV is a better deal.* PV stands for photovoltaics, a general term referring to the miracle by which panels made of nothing more exotic than highly refined sand are able to convert sunlight into electricity (see Figure 4-1). Back in the seventies, photovoltaic panels were far too expensive to compete with other kinds of alternative sources of energy — they were largely regarded as high-tech curiosities used by NASA to generate electricity for orbiting satellites and space stations.

Figure 4-1

A photovoltaic unit is a much more practical alternative energy source than wind machines.

In those not-so-long-ago days the only remotely viable alternative to the electric grid was wind power. It is actually painful now for me to re-read the literature from that era — the naivete about wind generators (to which I contributed my fair share) is almost childlike in its idealism. The fact is that we just didn't have enough experience with wind electric systems to justify our optimism.

To put it plainly: wind generators are viable options only at very specific locations — places so windy that few people would want to live there! I'm speaking of a ten to twelve mile per hour wind speed averaged over an entire year.

Yearly average wind speed means the sum of the mean wind speeds for each month divided by 12. Since this formula can be misleading — after all, using it one could come up with a ten mph "average" in an area where the wind blew 120 mph during March and not at all for the rest of the year — let me hasten to emphasize that the wind must average at least ten mph *every month of the year*. That crucial requirement probably leaves out most of the readers of this book, so I will confine much of my discussion in this chapter to photovoltaics.

In order to have a common ground of reference for this and subsequent chapters, let's first review some basics of electricity.

Volts, Amps and Watts

The three most important units of electrical measurement which concern us are: volts, amperes (amps) and watts. The easiest way to remember the difference between amps and volts is to think of amps as "current" which is measured in much the same way as the volume of water in a pipe is measured. If amps are volume, then volts can be thought of as "pressure" — the amount of push behind the volume of water. There's a world of difference between the flow of a swift mountain brook (high voltage, low amperage), and the flow of the sluggish waters of a large, slow-moving river (high amperage, low voltage). The analogy is not a perfect one, but it gives the essential concepts.

Obviously, the relationship between amps and volts is very important — the combination of the two when multiplied together is the total amount of electricity available, and is expressed as watts. Volts times amps equals watts. Thus, the electric volume of one ampere under the pressure of one volt means that one watt of power is available to do work. A 40 volt wind generator, such as one of the old Jacobs units, designed to produce 70 amps at full output is rated as a 2800 watt machine (40 x 70 = 2800).

Since watts are the measure of available energy, the very first thing that should concern us when considering any alternate energy device, such as a PV system or wind generator, is: How many watts is it capable of producing under the conditions for which you intend to use it? The easiest way to visualize the potential output of any given device is to imagine the number of one-hundred watt light bulbs it could theoretically light up at once. For example, a two-hundred watt generator can light only two one-hundred watt bulbs, while a 3000 watt generator will light thirty of them.

The Kilowatt Hour

Since a watt is a relatively small unit of power, electricity is usually described in terms of the kilowatt — a block of energy consisting of one-thousand watts. Even this term is relatively meaningless, however, unless it can be related to time. Hence, a kilowatt hour is the use of a given unit of electric power (one kilowatt) in relation to a given unit of time (one hour). One thousand watts used for one hour is equal to one kilowatt hour. Five-hundred watts used for two hours still adds up to one kilowatt hour, as does one watt for a thousand hours or two-thousand watts for one-half hour.

The electric company bases your monthly bill on the number of kilowatt hours you use during that period. If, during one month's time, you only burned a single hundred-watt bulb for a total of ten hours, you would be charged for one-hundred watts times ten hours, or one kilowatt hour. The electric meter automatically adds up the total number of kilowatt hours used. Obviously, this example is used only to illustrate a concept, since in actuality there is a minimum charge each month which is based upon more than a single kilowatt hour.

Battery Storage Systems

When one is using power generated by the wind or sun, it must be stored for use during times when the wind isn't blowing or the sun isn't shining. That means the wind generator or PV panel must be connected to a battery storage system. The most common battery used, and the only one I have experience with, is the lead-acid type.

Batteries used in home-power systems differ from automotive batteries in that they are designed for deep-cycling. That means that they can be almost completely discharged and still bounce back to their full capacity when charged up again. An automotive battery is not designed for this kind of use, and will be quickly ruined if subjected to such treatment. Deep-cycle batteries designed for stationary power systems and golf carts are the type to consider.

There are many different battery configurations. Most commercial/industrial stationary power systems (such as those maintained by the telephone company) use very large capacity two-volt cells hooked up in series to equal the voltage of the system. Thus a twelve-volt system will consist of six two-volt batteries; a twenty-four volt system would contain twelve of them. I once owned a thirty-two volt Jacobs wind-electric system which fed sixteen two-volt cells. They were huge things, weighing over a hundred pounds apiece, which I bought surplus from the Los Alamos salvage yard. Unfortunately, battery bargains like these are no longer available as salvage, due to current government regulations on the sale of anything containing lead.

Figure 4-2

The large, six-volt batteries store the energy generated by my six PV panels and one Wincharger.

Other configurations are possible. I currently power a small office/guest-house with six large six-volt batteries hooked in both series and parallel to make twelve volts. These are fed by six 40-watt PV panels and one 200-watt Wincharger. On a sunny and windy day it doesn't take long to fill them to capacity, particularly since I presently don't draw on the system for more than lights, a domestic water pump, a small stereo and a computer. With the exception of the pump, these are all low-wattage items which draw little power from the system. I deliberately over-sized my battery capacity to cover those relatively rare winter blizzards when we can have several days in a row without sunlight. The wind generator was salvaged from the old *Survival Greenhouse* for nostalgia's sake — by itself, it seldom provides dependable power, but I still love to hear it whirring in the breeze!

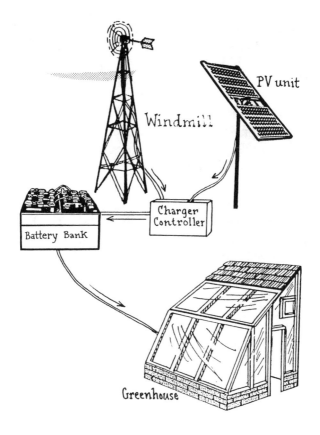

Figure 4-3

Schematic for an alternative energy system using PV collector and storage batteries.

Weak Links and Current Thoughts

Now the original Survival Greenhouse was "designed" to get all of its power (for aerating the fish tank, heating its water in a solar panel, and operating winter grow-lights) from that little 12-volt generator. Because I'd had no experience with wind electric systems and their utter dependence on a high average wind speed, I didn't know that the tiny Wincharger (through no fault of its own) would prove to be the weakest link in the whole system. However, by the time that PV became affordable, I'd already abandoned both my original concept of aquaculture, and trying to grow plants in deep winter. The only other need for power became apparent when I adopted the NFT hydroponic system, but that design uses so little electricity, that one would be hard pressed to justify the expense of a PV system to accommodate it.

The respective chapters on those subjects will provide the relevant details. The upshot of this chapter is that while photovoltaics are wonderful sources of energy, our modified greenhouse eco-system doesn't really need them.

5

Greenhouse
Temperature Control

Of course, all greenhouses are solar in that they make use of the sun, but our definition is that of Fisher and Yanda in their book **The Food and Heat Producing Solar Greenhouse.** *That is, a solar greenhouse incorporates three basic elements: efficient collection of solar energy, storage of solar energy, and the prevention of heat loss.*

— Tom Gross, *New Mexico Solar Energy Assn. Bulletin,* July, 1977

All greenhouses are placed within one of three separate temperature ranges — the *cool* greenhouse, with a range of 40 to

55 degrees Fahrenheit; the *moderate* greenhouse at 55 to 65 degrees Fahrenheit; and the *warm* greenhouse in the 65 to 75 degree range. These figures represent minimum night time temperatures — the lowest the greenhouse can be allowed to go and still remain in its category. Taylor and Gregg inform us that:

> The word "greenhouse" originally implied a cool greenhouse as differing from a hothouse, or stove. In the old books, plants requiring a high temperature were called "stove" plants.

Obviously, each plant variety grows best within a specific range of temperatures, and since we are trying to eliminate fossil fuels as a heat source in our ideal greenhouse, it will probably fall into the cool or moderate category. This puts a natural restriction on the kinds of plants we can grow. However, since most readers of this book are probably only interested in the usual North American vegetables, this doesn't pose much of a problem.

Figure 5-1 shows the pertinent mean temperatures for each of the zodiacal months of the 1973-1974 year — which was a typical season in this area. The average low temperatures are graphed in Figure 5-2. As you can see, the magical 40 degrees Fahrenheit *low* temperature does not appear until Aries (March 21 to April 21). As mentioned earlier, however, I found that cool weather plants (lettuce, spinach, etc.) began to thrive a full month earlier — around February 21st. The attentive reader will also note that the mean temperature for Scorpio (October 21 to November 21) is 41 degrees F. — in theory, a temperature capable of providing another month of growing beyond the October 21st cut-off point. The fact that plant growth is negligible during this period indicates the effects of a waning photoperiod. This very important consideration will be considered in some depth in the next chapter.

1974 GREENHOUSE DATA

	Month	Greenhouse Temperatures			Outside Temperatures		
		Low Average	High Average	Mean	Low Average	High Average	Mean
Winter	Capricorn	30	58	44	15	51	33
	Aquarius	31	72	51	14	55	34
	Pisces	39	86	62	24	57	40
Spring	Aries	40	94	67	26	59	42
	Taurus	49	99	74	37	73	55
	Gemini	55	99	77	46	82	64
Summer	Cancer	57	103	80	53	88	70
	Leo	58	90	74	52	83	67
	Virgo	57	90	73	47	80	63
Autumn	Libra	52	90	71	40	73	56
	Scorpio	41	80	60	28	67	47
	Sagittarius	29	73	51	16	64	40

ZODIACAL MONTHS

Capricorn	=	Dec./Jan.	Cancer =	June/July
Aquarius	=	Jan./Feb.	Leo =	July/Aug.
Pisces	=	Feb./Mar.	Virgo =	Aug./Sept.
Aries	=	Mar./April	Libra =	Sept./Oct.
Taurus	=	April/May	Scorpio =	Oct./Nov.
Gemini	=	May/June	Sagittarius =	Nov./Dec.

Figure 5-1

1974 greenhouse and outdoor temperatures contrasted.

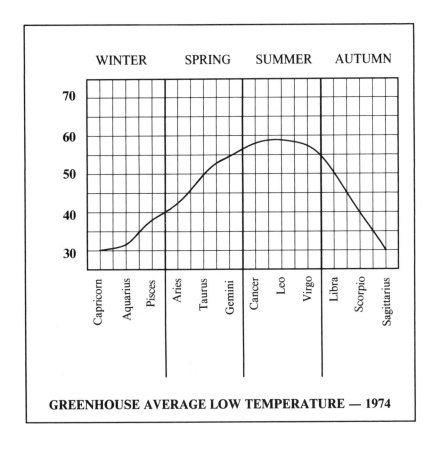

GREENHOUSE AVERAGE LOW TEMPERATURE — 1974

Figure 5-2

This graph shows the average low temperatures for the greenhouse in 1974. Alternative-energy growing is not efficient when average lows are below 40 degrees F.

The Hi-Lo Thermometer

Essential to any greenhouse is a high/low thermometer. This is an ingenious device which will record the highest and lowest temperatures during any given period. It is also useful to have an identical thermometer outside the greenhouse. In this way, one can keep records of the daily high and low temperatures, inside and outside, throughout the yearly cycle. After you've done this for a year, you'll begin to understand your local eco-system much better, and be able to intelligently plan your planting dates. After two years of making these records, an intuition begins to form in your consciousness, and you'll understand how so-called peasant and primitive farmers "know" when the optimum time has come to plant, cultivate and harvest. There is no magic in this — it is just being in tune with your environment.

Cooling — Ventilation

High greenhouse temperatures — anything above 90 degrees F. — are as much to be avoided as temperatures below 40 degrees F. In warm weather, the greenhouse must be cooled. The conventional greenhouse operator uses elaborate air conditioning equipment to accomplish this — all of it dependent upon fossil fuels. Since the eco-system concept rules out such devices, we must rely on natural methods only.

I've found that during hot weather the vents and door can generally be left open all of the time without undue trauma to the plants. At this altitude, ventilation becomes a serious problem only during two or three weeks in late June and early July, during the zodiacal month of Cancer. While it is true that the squash and tomatoes sometimes wilted during the heat of the day, so did their brothers and sisters outside in the garden. Be aware also, that the conventional greenhouse books are usually speaking of flowering plants, many of which are exotic tropical and semi-tropical varieties specific only to certain environments, and requiring a great deal of care and attention. Our focus here is on the homely tomatoes, cucumbers, squash and lettuce common to most gardens in the United States.

Generally, most solar greenhouse designs provide a low vent for incoming air on the east wall, and a high vent for outgoing air on the west wall. Since warm air rises and cool air sinks, this ventilation placement creates a natural convection current which keeps the air moving in the greenhouse without recourse to electric fans or other energy-intensive forms of cooling.

Unfortunately, such low-tech, manually operated ventilation systems require that someone be present throughout the day to adjust them for changing weather conditions. Particularly critical times are early in the season when sudden high winds can make a warm April morning seem like a cold and blustery February dusk. It doesn't take long to damage or even kill young plants under such circumstances.

Automatic Ventilators

An automatic ventilator opener/closer which uses no energy other than sunlight has been developed in recent years. (See the "Access" section at the end of this chapter.) Working on the principle of a captive temperature-sensitive gas expanding and contracting in a cylinder, these devices automatically compensate for fluctuations in warmth throughout the day — opening and closing the vents at adjustable, predetermined values (see Figure 5-3). My experience with these devices has been confined to those in my recently purchased free-standing fiberglass greenhouse. They work fine in stable weather, but I find that mine were not designed to compensate for sudden winds — to the point that the shafts inside each cylinder have been seriously bent when high gusts have caught them extended and vulnerable. This made it necessary to detach the cylinders and operate the vents manually during the windy season.

Figure 5-3

Solar-powered automatic ventilators adjust window openings according to fluctuations in temperatures.

Cooling — Shading

In addition to ventilation, shading the greenhouse can lower inside temperatures as much as ten degrees or more during hot weather. Shading materials can range from simple fences made of bamboo slats to strategically planted deciduous trees. (Leaves provide shade in the summer when it is required, and their absence during the colder part of the year allows the sun's rays to enter when they're most needed.) I once tried growing pole beans over the greenhouse, but found that they didn't grow quite fast enough to shade the structure during the hottest part of the season.

While our high average greenhouse temperature for the month of Cancer, 1974, was a stifling 103 degrees F., the plants survived in good order, with no obvious deficiency symptoms other than leaf wilting during the hottest part of each day. The tomatoes and cucumbers seemed to thrive in such an environment, though common sense, plus all of the greenhouse books, will tell us that temperatures over 90 degrees F. are not desirable. In my experience, shading, plus natural ventilation, is usually sufficient to keep the greenhouse reasonably cool during hot weather.

Heating

Keeping the greenhouse warm in cold weather has been more of a problem for me than keeping it cool in hot weather. Even the insulating properties of the earth cannot protect a pit greenhouse from freezing temperatures in mid-winter. Although my pit greenhouse was in the *cool* 40 degree category, it proved to be difficult to hold onto even that relatively low temperature range at night during January.

Heating strategies for forcing structures usually break down into three categories: auxiliary sources of warmth, insulation, and passive storage. As mentioned, conventional greenhouses have traditionally made use of fossil fuels for winter heat — usually natural gas, heating oil, or even electricity (the most inefficient, in terms of energy usage, of all common heating methods).

The Wood Stove

Perhaps the simplest auxiliary heat source which doesn't burn non-renewable fuels is the wood-burning stove. In this regard, modern thermostatically controlled units, such as the Ashley automatic heater, would be the most efficient choice.

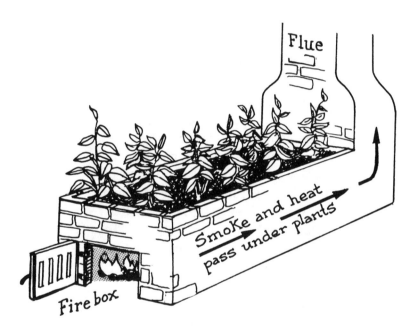

Figure 5-4

The heating system in the historic Waltham, Massachusetts greenhouse.

The original Waltham, Massachusetts, pit greenhouse made use of an ingenious heating system which insured that the soil temperature in the greenhouse was always adequate for the plants under cultivation. As I understand it, the plants grew in a raised bed which had a chimney flue running beneath it for its entire length. A firebox at one end of the flue was stoked with enough wood to last the night, thus maintaining adequate heat in the greenhouse soil to raise tropical and semitropical plants through the cold New England winters. Reportedly, they even grew bananas in this fashion! Obviously, these greenhouse gardeners of almost two centuries ago were making use of the fact that high soil temperatures can compensate for low air temperatures. (See Figure 5-4.)

Insulation

Insulation is an essential component of any energy-efficient structure; it creates a buffer for the normally fluctuating temperature extremes encountered during the diurnal/nocturnal cycle. For example, inside daytime highs in the seventies and eighties in January are routinely followed by below-zero lows at night in my uninsulated freestanding greenhouse. Depending on the weather, the inside temperature will often soar far above that outside, but at night it always drops to within a few degrees of the outside low. This is because this greenhouse is both un-heated and has no insulation.

Insulation — Air-lock Doorway

One insulating feature which can be added to any greenhouse design is an air-lock entrance. This is simply a double doorway and vestibule which prevents frigid outside blasts of air from shocking the plants every time someone enters or leaves the greenhouse. In addition, commercial tomato growers often use this vestibule as a decontamination area — a place to change shoes or clothing to prevent infection from such plant diseases as Tobacco Mosaic Virus. (Anyone who smokes is a potential carrier of this affliction which is devastating to tomato plants.)

Insulation — Greenhouse Plastic

Methods of insulation can take many different forms. To begin with, it is generally accepted that plastic-covered greenhouses are somewhat more efficient heat retainers than glass-covered structures. It is further held as true that a double layer of plastic is up to forty percent more efficient than a single layer alone. The air trapped between the two layers is an extremely effective insulating buffer which protects the greenhouse from outside freezing temperatures. (Double layers of glass are nearly as efficient, and as we shall see later on, may be a better choice in the long run.)

One of the interesting features of the original Lama Grow Hole (it evolved somewhat over the years), was that it was triple-glazed — that is, the top and bottom layers consisted of the ubiquitous vinyl sheets which enclosed a middle layer of Air-cap D-120 — the plastic "bubble" sheeting commonly used as packing material for fragile merchandise. In theory, this inner stratum of vinyl bubbles should have provided tremendous insulating value. With hindsight, I suspect that the three plastic layers probably blocked a lot of light — I've never heard of the results of the technique, and neither have I heard of anyone ever trying it again.

In addition, while these materials are inexpensive and readily available, their effective life is very short — most vinyl plastic turns yellow and brittle with age, and cannot be expected to last for much more than one growing season.

A more permanent type of plastic is a special greenhouse material made of fiberglass, commonly called *Filon* or *Lascolite*. These are just two of several trade names. I've used them both, and despite proprietary claims to the contrary, I found that as far as the user is concerned the actual materials differ about as much as Fords and Chevrolets (i.e., it's a matter of personal preference which one you use).

There are different types and thicknesses of this fiberglass material, some of it with an advertised life expectancy of over fifteen years. I used *Filon* on my first greenhouse; it came in three 4′ x 24′ rolls which I purchased through the Sears catalog. I didn't install it in a double layer, however. During the winter of 1974 I put up a sheet of the much cheaper vinyl plastic on the inside of the greenhouse — this was an experiment to determine the effectiveness of the doubled layer. During 1975 I didn't use the vinyl and was thereby convinced of its usefulness — in 1974, the mean low temperatures in Capricorn and Aquarius had been 30 and 31 degrees F. respectively. During the same period in 1975, with similar outside temperatures, the mean low temperatures were 22 and 27 degrees F. without the extra layer of plastic — an average difference of between 4 and 8 degrees. Double-layering, then, is worth the extra trouble and expense if you are serious about growing in deep winter.

Some Drawbacks of Fiberglass

It is probable that fiberglass greenhouse materials have been improved significantly since the 1970's, so what I now have to say about them should be evaluated with that in mind.

To put it bluntly, I generally dislike fiberglass. My 1974-vintage *Filon* began turning yellow far sooner than the advertised fifteen years, and started showing signs of structural degradation within five years. It wasn't long before the eroding surface began to expose the inner glass fibers to weather and sunlight, and soon I had what looked like a sleazy, high-tech slum building.

In fairness, however, I must add that these objections are purely aesthetic — the light-emitting and heat-retaining properties of the fiberglass seemed quite unaffected by the degradation process, and this is undoubtedly what is referred to in the fifteen-year estimate of life expectancy.

Nevertheless, I definitely prefer double-paned glass to fiberglass. Although it is initially more expensive, it is far easier to live with over the years. This personal prejudice applies to all plastic greenhouse materials — in my opinion, the trouble of putting up the vinyl sheeting is hardly worth whatever increased growth it might provide in deep winter. I am in good company in my prejudices:

> We use a lot of polyethylene, vinyl and other products of the same ilk, but we don't like them. Poverty dictated that we use these "cheap" substances but we are beginning to realize that there was a lot of false economy involved. Plastic is relatively cheap but it is forever being replaced and after a few years one begins to conclude that one would have been much further ahead to use materials that last a lifetime, or longer.
>
> — *The Book of the New Alchemists,* 1977

Since the time that these biases were being formed, a new type of rigid greenhouse plastic, available in double-glazed acrylic panels of various sizes, has come on the market. The brand I have heard about is called *Exolite.* (See the "Access" section at the end of this chapter.) Reputedly, this material is not subject to the degradation problems of the products mentioned earlier. Since I have no experience with it, I cannot do more than mention its availability.

Beadwall Insulation

An initially promising idea developed back in the seventies by the Zomeworks Corporation was the Beadwall Insulation System. This consisted of an appropriately sized module made of a double layer of glass separated by about two or three inches of air space. At one end of the module was a hole connecting it to a storage container filled with styrofoam beads. A reversible vacuum cleaner motor was placed between the glass "sandwich" and the storage container. At night, when insulation was required, the motor would blow the styrofoam beads into the space between the two pieces of glass until it was filled completely, thus providing an excellent buffer against the cold; in the morning, the motor was reversed and the beads were sucked back into the storage container. In theory, the idea was an elegant solution to the problems of winter greenhouse temperature control.

In practice however, the beads eventually began to disintegrate — each time they were blown from one location to the other, tiny dust particles were worn off each piece of styrofoam; static electricity then caused this dust to cling to the glass, eventually resulting in an unsightly and light-blocking film which was impossible to clean off because it was inside the sandwich. An excellent idea thus proved to be better than the material available to implement it.

Insulation Panels

Insulation can take many different forms other than the double layer. The Taylor-Gregg pit greenhouse didn't make use of either double-paned glass or auxiliary heat, relying instead on insulation panels which were placed over the glass in the evenings and removed each morning — except, of course, during inclement weather when the insulation was left on. It has been estimated that insulation panels can cut night-time heat losses by as much as sixty percent, and need be nothing more exotic than burlap sacks full of leaves or sawdust.

I can attest to the tremendous difference that a few inches of "insulation" will make in greenhouse heat retention. During the coldest part of the winter of 1974 the temperature plunged to

5 degrees below 0 one night. The inside greenhouse temperature was a "balmy" 34 degrees F. — entering the greenhouse that morning from the frigid outdoors felt like stepping into a heated room, and actually steamed up my glasses. The reason was ten inches of snow on the greenhouse roof — relatively speaking, a very effective insulator.

Figure 5-5

The Steve Baer home, Albuquerque, NM, circa 1973, showing the reflecting insulation panels in open mode.

All things being equal, the efficient use of both double-paned glass or plastic in conjunction with insulation panels should enable one to maintain the winter mean low temperature at or above the magic 40 degrees F. required for the cool greenhouse. Some growers use removable double-plastic modules, similar to "storm windows," which are easily mounted against the glazing. In addition, one could utilize opaque panels made of styrofoam (or any good insulating material), for placement either inside or outside of the greenhouse at night and when the weather is cold and cloudy. (Although an excellent insulating material, styrofoam panels should always be laminated with light plywood or sturdy cardboard, with the edges securely taped, or otherwise sealed, because the bare material crumbles easily and leaves little statically-charged white beads everywhere.)

One excellent technique of combining heat and light transfer with insulation is to attach hinged panels to the front of the greenhouse which are painted reflective white on their inner-facing surfaces. That way, when lowered during the daytime, they bounce an amazing amount of sunlight into the greenhouse, and when raised at night provide an insulating buffer from the freezing night air. I first saw this technique used by Steve Baer, founder of Zomeworks, who used such panels to reflect solar energy into his home, where it was captured and retained overnight in black, water-filled drums. (See Figure 5-5.)

Passive Heat Storage

Which brings us to the last category of greenhouse heat retention — one which doesn't naturally fall under either insulation or auxiliary heat. Usually referred to as "passive" solar heating, this is the utilization of an inert heat storage medium such as water or rocks to absorb the high daytime temperatures and hold them overnight. Even in deep winter, high daytime mean temperatures can reach into the seventies and above — well above the necessary 40 degree F. minimum for meaningful plant growth. The question is, how can we hold onto that warmth and keep it from dissipating after sunset?

Many early solar houses, often with attached greenhouses as their primary heat source, utilized fifty-five gallon drums of water (painted black to absorb heat) as passive storage systems. Since those pioneer days of solar experimentation, other, more aesthetic containers have been developed. Tanks made of fiberglass, less "industrial" in appearance than oil drums and available in many sizes, are now available for water storage in greenhouses. (See the "Access" section at the end of this chapter.) They also make great aquaculture tanks, thus doing double duty — providing space for another food crop while balancing heat fluctuations in the winter greenhouse.

The original conception of my eco-system was a little more complicated (and a great deal less elegant) than that. It called for a solar panel through which the fish tank water could be *actively* circulated. The idea is reasonably sound, providing one has a steady and reliable source of power, but I found that for it to work, a solar collector of at least one-hundred square feet would be required to keep the fourteen-hundred gallon tank at an effective temperature. Roughly, that would necessitate a collector the size of three 4 x 8 sheets of plywood. At that time, the off-the-shelf cost of such a system was far beyond my means, and although I could have built my own collector without much trouble or expense, I soon came upon another limiting factor which prevented my pursuing the project. The 12-volt, 66-watt bilge pump I was using to circulate the fish tank water was not nearly powerful enough to push liquid through 100 square feet of solar collector. A pump large enough to handle the job would have required far more power than the monthly twenty-kilowatt hour maximum that I could even optimistically expect from my wind electric system. Thus I learned that "passive," rather than "active" (energy consuming) solar systems, are always more compatible with eco-system concepts.

To provide an off-the-shelf active wind and solar energy package adequate to my original design would have cost far in excess of a conventional greenhouse heating system. I didn't realize it at that time, but the utilization of double glazing, passive heat storage and insulation panels was the truly ecological solution to these problems.

Even so, considering the fact that growing a meaningful crop of vegetable produce in deep winter is impractical in most areas outside of the tropics, these considerations become somewhat academic in reference to anything but an attached greenhouse used as an auxiliary heat source for one's dwelling.

Access

Automatic Ventilators
Thermofor Automatic Window Opener
Thermoforce Ltd
Unit 4 C, Tetbury Industrial Estate
Tetbury, Glos., GL-8 8E2
Great Britain

Bayliss Autovents
Compton,
Ashbourne, Derbyshire, DE6 1DA
Great Britain

Greenhouse Plastic
Exolite 16/32
Cyro Industries
Woodcliff Lake, NJ 07675

Fiberglass Tanks
Energy Saver's Catalog
Solar Components Corp.
121 Valley St.
Manchester, NH 03103

6

Photoperiod

Photoperiod: the relative lengths of alternating periods of lightness and darkness as they affect the growth and maturity of an organism (as in the effect upon the flowering of plants and the breeding of animals).

— *Webster's Third New International Dictionary*

In late summer, have you ever noticed that the leaves of certain trees begin changing to their autumn colors before the first frost? This phenomenon illustrates the effects of a waning photoperiod — the amount of light which is available for a plant to carry out its primary function of photosynthesis. Some plant species are so specialized in their light requirements that even one less hour of sunlight per day will trigger the beginning of their dormant cycle.

Regarding winter photoperiods, Ernest Chabot, in his book *Greenhouse Gardening for Everyone*, states:

> Perhaps you're asking, "why not grow these fruits under glass in winter as well as summer?" Of course you can, but the expense for additional heat and the slow production when days are short would hardly make them profitable in a small greenhouse.

Canadian agricultural bulletin No. 1460, *Soilless Culture of Commercial Greenhouse Tomatoes*, tells us that:

> The fall crop is harvested in October, November, and early December. Production beyond this date is not economical owing to high costs of heating, insufficient daylight, and slow development and ripening of fruit.

Cathey and Campbell, in "Lamps and lighting — a horticultural view," an article in the November 1974 issue of *Lighting Design and Application,* explain further:

> In the winter, most plants in greenhouses in northern latitudes do not receive enough light to maintain the growth characteristics that are possible during the rest of the year. Limitation of light reduces the photosynthetic activity of the plants.

The reason I have quoted at length on this subject is to emphasize something that many people do not take into consideration — we all know that greenhouses must be kept *warm* in the wintertime, but relatively few of us consider the problem of insufficient *light* when the days are short.

Another glance at Figure 2-1 reminds us that the *effective growing season* ends October 21st, and doesn't begin again until somewhere around the 21st of February. The limiting factors are both temperature and photoperiod. Thus, even if one is able to maintain sufficient heat in the greenhouse during the winter, plant growth will still be inadequate because of the lack of available light.

Wittwer and Honma, in *Greenhouse Tomatoes — Guidelines for Successful Production,* go so far as to say:

> The technology for maintaining a greenhouse tomato crop in which harvest begins in the fall and continues at a profitable level of productivity through the winter is not yet available.

If even commercial growers with "efficient" fossil fuel heating and lighting systems consider winter greenhouse production to be uneconomical, how can we, with only the low energy of the natural systems available to us, expect to make it a worthwhile endeavor? Realistically, it may not be feasible, but there are a few possibilities to be explored before a final decision can be made.

The Three Qualities of Light

There are three qualities of light which are important for us to consider. All three act together to facilitate efficient plant growth. They are:

1. Intensity of light;
2. Duration of light;
3. Spectral content of light.

The *intensity* of sunlight is at its weakest in the wintertime because the low angle of the sun in the sky causes its radiation to pass obliquely through the atmosphere, where it is deflected and absorbed by dust and other particles. In addition, because of this lower angle, winter days are shorter, which affects light *duration.* As long as it comes from the sun, of course, the *spectral content* of the light remains the same all year long and is not a problem unless we decide to supplement our solar intensity and duration with artificial lighting.

Light Intensity — Reflectors

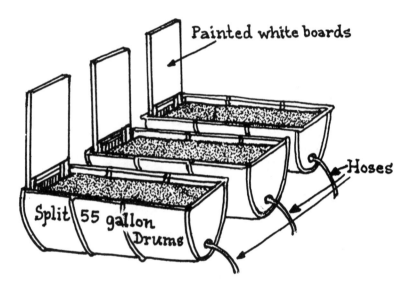

Figure 6-1

Reflectors painted with flat white paint and placed behind the beds significantly help plant growth in the early growing season.

Light intensity can be substantially increased by placing reflectors behind the plants (see Figure 6-1). I proved this to myself during the early spring of 1975, when I placed a board covered with aluminum foil behind some Chinese cabbage seedlings. Another group of identical seedlings had no reflector. Within one week the seedlings receiving the additional reflected light were measurably larger than the control group. Within two weeks, the difference in the sizes of the two groups of plants was enough to suggest that they had been planted several weeks apart!

Reflectors are very useful items in greenhouse gardening, and recent research has shown that white mylar plastic and even flat white paint are better surfaces than aluminum foil. In fact, strange as it may seem, aluminum foil actually tests out as a very poor reflector for the promotion of plant growth. It worked for me before I knew better, but a white painted surface would have been considerably more efficient.

There is a point of diminishing returns from the use of reflected light, however. This was reached later in the season when other plants started with reflectors showed no differences from those without them. The explanation for this phenomenon is quoted from the *Encyclopedia Britannica*:

> Over a range of moderate temperatures and at low to medium light intensities (relative to the normal range of the plant species), the rate of photosynthesis increases as the (light) intensity increases and is independent of temperature. As the light intensity increases to higher levels, however, the rate becomes increasingly dependent upon temperature and less dependent upon intensity; light "saturation" is achieved at a specific light intensity, and the rate then is dependent only on temperature if all other factors are constant.

This explains why plant growth after February 21st suddenly begins to prosper, even though the greenhouse temperatures are still relatively low: the days have gotten long enough so that the solar intensity and duration are within the range of the plants' photoperiodic response.

Light Duration

Reflectors, of course, only increase light intensity, not duration. Therefore, in mid-winter a reflector alone is not enough to bring plant growth up to summer norms. What is needed is a means of extending the short winter day to a length at least equal to a summer day.

The table of photoperiods (see Figure 6-2) shows the day lengths on the solstices and equinoxes in four United States latitudes.

PHOTOPERIODS IN THE UNITED STATES			
	Winter (Dec. 21)	Spring (Mar. 21) Autumn (Sept. 21)	Summer (June 21)
(1) 45° N. Latitude	8 hrs. 46 min.	12 hrs. 17 min	15 hrs. 37 min.
(2) 40° N. Latitude	9 hrs. 20 min.	12 hrs. 15 min.	15 hrs. 1 min.
(3) 35° N. Latitude	9 hrs. 48 min.	12 hrs. 14 min.	14 hrs. 31 min.
(4) 30° N. Latitude	10 hrs. 13 min.	12 hrs. 12 min.	14 hrs. 5 min.

    (1)   45° N. Lat. = Portland, Oregon; Minneapolis; Bangor

    (2)   40° N. Lat. = Salt Lake City; Denver; Philadelphia

    (3)   35° N. Lat. = Santa Barbara; Albuquerque; Memphis

    (4)   30° N. Lat. = Houston; New Orleans; Jacksonville

Figure 6-2

Photoperiods at four United States latitudes.

At my location, roughly thirty-five degrees North Latitude, we receive a little less than ten hours of daylight on December 21st, the winter solstice. Since we know that our effective growing season ends around the 21st of October, we can interpolate from the table that any day-length of less than eleven hours is inadequate for proper plant growth. The intensity and duration of light is below the level of photoperiodic response that millions of years of evolution have built into most of the vegetables we are interested in raising. Plants evolved in the natural world, not in greenhouses, and we must provide them with the environmental conditions they require if we expect to grow much food during the "night-time" portion of the yearly cycle.

While light intensity may be boosted with reflectors, light duration can only be increased by using an artificial light source such as fluorescent tubes. Since I know that a winter day at this latitude is about ten hours long, I would only need to burn lights for a total of four hours a day during December to give the plants the photoperiodic equivalent of a day in June. This could easily be accomplished with a timing device which would turn the lights on two hours before sunrise, off at dawn, and on again for two more hours after sunset. Or, alternatively, because the intensity of the solar radiation (heat and light) is highest in the afternoon, the lights could be turned on just before dusk and remain on for at least four hours to maintain a high light level at the end of the day when the plants are already "awake" and hopefully already photosynthesizing at near-peak levels.

Fluorescent Lighting

Supplemental illumination in greenhouses increases photosynthesis. Cost of power, however, makes this impractical for all but crops of the highest value. Fluorescent lights are the most efficient for photosynthesis.

— *Encyclopedia Britannica*

In terms of increasing photoperiod in the winter greenhouse, the energy efficiency of the fluorescent tube, plus the fact that it produces wavelengths which are beneficial to plant growth, make it ideal for use with the low power output of PV or wind

generated electricity. It is a happy fact that, watt for watt,
fluorescent tubes emit more than twice the amount of light that
incandescents do. The heat output is about the same, but since
the heat is spread over such a large area the total effect is one
of "coolness." This enables us to put fluorescent lights very close
to the plants without danger of burning them. Most fluorescent
light gardeners use a standard fixture of four forty-watt tubes,
which draws one-hundred and sixty watts (4 x 40 = 160). Using
one-hundred and sixty watts for four hours (the length of time
to bring our photoperiod to the equivalent of a day in June)
equals six-hundred and forty watt-hours of power used each day
(160 x 4 = 640). If the lights are used at this rate for a month,
we will consume 19.2 kilowatt hours every thirty days (640 x
30 = 19200). This is really pushing the generating capacity of
most any alternative power system we'd be likely to use, so we'll
have to look at other lighting options.

Other Fluorescent Possibilities

Three forty-watt fluorescent tubes used according to the afore-
mentioned schedule would only draw 14.4 kilowatt hours a
month, and two tubes only 9.6 kilowatt hours. Of course, each
tube subtracted from service reduces the light intensity, but if
used in conjunction with reflectors behind and beneath the plant,
the loss could be minimized. There is evidence to indicate that
plants are able to respond to light from beneath their leaves as
well as from above; thus, a white plastic "mulch" around each
plant would reflect light up under the leaves for increased
intensity.

Foot-candles

Light intensity is measured in foot-candles, and it is important
that the tubes be placed close enough to the plant to provide the

proper strength of illumination. Since fluorescent tubes are relatively cool, they can be put within four inches or less of the plants without danger of burning them. Most experts seem in agreement that a light intensity of at least one-thousand foot-candles is best for maximum growth. The chart (Figure 6-3), taken from *The Encyclopedia of Organic Gardening* (Rodale, 1972), gives the foot-candle to plant distance ratios for two standard forty-watt tubes with a reflector at the light source.

1 inch from lights	1,000 foot candles
2 inches from lights	950 foot candles
3 inches from lights	750 foot candles
4 inches from lights	650 foot candles
5 inches from lights	560 foot candles
6 inches from lights	460 foot candles
7 inches from lights	430 foot candles
8 inches from lights	370 foot candles
9 inches from lights	360 foot candles
10 inches from lights	350 foot candles

Figure 6-3

Light intensity in foot-candles at various distances from source.

Of course, since light intensity varies inversely with the square of the distance from the source, a small change in light distance from the plants will make a very large change in the number of foot-candles received.

Grow Lights

At this point it should be pointed out that although special fluorescent "Grow Lights" are available at a higher price than conventional tubes, they apparently offer no significant advantages. In my research on the subject I have found that most experts recommend a half and half combination of "Warm White" and "Cool White" tubes. The extra expense of the special Grow Lights is not commensurate with their plant growing ability.

Spectral Content of Light

As briefly mentioned before, the spectral content of light is very important to proper plant growth. We know that white light is made up of all of the colors of the spectrum, and that each color is distinguished by its own wave length. These wave lengths of light are measured in angstrom units — one angstrom unit being one-hundred-millionth of a centimeter long. Scientists have determined that plants particularly respond to red light at 6500 angstrom units, and to blue light at 4500 angstrom units. The red end of the spectrum promotes flowering in plants, and the blue end is necessary for foliage growth. Generally, fluorescent tubes are high in blue light, and incandescent bulbs are high in red light.

Many artificial light gardeners mix fluorescent and incandescent illumination to provide a balance of both red and blue light. Used as a supplement to daylight in the winter greenhouse, however, fluorescent tubes alone should be adequate. This is because the winter greenhouse crop should logically consist of cool-weather plants such as lettuce, spinach, Swiss Chard, Chinese Cabbage, etc. — plants which are grown for their foliage rather than their fruit. Warm weather crops — those generally raised for their fruits, such as tomatoes, cucumbers, squash, etc. — cannot be grown efficiently in an unheated eco-system greenhouse during the winter because they require minimum temperatures of at least 60 degrees F. Since red light is most necessary to fruit-producing plants, it need not concern us too much — we want all the blue light we can get to increase the foliage on our winter lettuce and spinach. Actually, a mixture of warm-white and cool-white fluorescent tubes should provide an adequate balance of red and blue wave-lengths. (Experiments with blue and red filters placed over a large growing space to alter the color of daylight may have interesting results.)

As absorbing as all this is, we are still faced with the fact that increasing our photoperiod with artificial lights in a greenhouse using only natural energy systems, such as PV or wind, is impractical unless we can bring down the number of kilowatt hours consumed to match their lower output. Here's one method that might work:

Cyclic Lighting

Cathey and Campbell, in the article cited earlier in this chapter, mention some very interesting experiments with photoperiod control which have tremendous implications for those of us restricted to the relatively low power output provided by alternate energy systems. I have not yet tried these methods, so mention them here only to acquaint the reader with their existence:

> Techniques were developed in the late fifties to reduce the electrical energy requirements for photoperiod control. ...The technique was based on repeating light-dark cycles over several hours during the middle of a long night. ...We have observed that ten to twenty foot-candles from incandescent-filament lamps, thirty seconds on and thirty seconds off all night, promoted the early flowering of

China Aster, Hyoscyamus, Petunia, Snapdragon, Sugar Beet, and tuberous-rooted Begonia. The use of artificial lights to promote the continued vegetative growth of woody plants is relatively easy to obtain with cyclic lighting. ...It means that three minutes of light every thirty minutes or six seconds every sixty seconds for the middle four hours of a sixteen hour dark period promote the continued vegetative growth of most woody plants.

As is usual in much of the greenhouse literature, flowers and ornamentals are the plant types most often referred to, so it appears that there is much research yet to be done with vegetable crops. The results of the above techniques are very promising, however, and the energy efficiency of cyclic lighting just may be the key to making winter greenhouse gardening economical.

If a four tube, one-hundred and sixty watt fluorescent fixture was turned on for fifteen minutes every hour during the middle four hours of the winter night (a simple timer could accomplish this), only 160 watt-hours would be consumed each day. This adds up to only 4.8 kilowatt hours every thirty days — a relatively insignificant amount of electricity, even by photovoltaic and wind-electric standards.

The reader is also asked to note that some of the light intensities in the above experiments were as low as ten footcandles — a hundred times less intense than the thousand footcandles recommended by most artificial light gardening manuals. The technique of cyclic lighting appears to hold much promise.

Update: 1991

In researching the latest literature on photoperiod control for the revised edition of this book I was led to some fascinating data coming from probably the only growers with a crop valuable enough to rationalize the expense of full artificial lighting: the indoor marijuana cultivators. Although it is not within the scope of this book to cover this subject, the curious reader may be interested in the truly amazing production figures attainable with modern High Intensity Discharge (HID) lamps. While in no way compatible with the eco-system philosophy (HID lamps are typically in the 1000-watt range), the techniques developed by these growers make fascinating reading, and go to prove that with enough electricity one can do almost anything. The reference I have is: *Indoor Marijuana Horticulture,* by Jorge Cervantes, Van Patten, 4204 SE Ogden, Portland, Oregon 97206, 1990. ISBN 0-932331-01-7.

Adequate temperature and photoperiod are only two of the requirements that plants need for carrying out photosynthesis. Carbon dioxide is a third necessity that is often overlooked by home greenhouse gardeners.

7

Carbon Dioxide

Inflated plastic greenhouses have been built, costing only about 15 cents per square foot, near the fishing community of Puerto Penasco on the Gulf of California. This location provides bright and plentiful sunlight almost every day of the year, but this is coupled with almost a complete absence of fresh water. The enclosed plants are grown in an atmosphere of approximately 100 percent relative humidity and 1,000 ppm. of carbon dioxide (the normal outdoor figure is 300), thereby reducing the water requirements to 1 to 5 percent of normal.

— S.H. Wittwer, "Food Supply: the Fruits of Research,"
Technology Review, March 1969

Earlier we quoted a phrase from the *Encyclopedia Britannica;* to give ourselves a point of departure for this chapter, it bears repeating:

> The amount of *light*, the *carbon dioxide* supply, and the *temperature* are the three most important factors that directly affect the rate of photosynthesis; *water* and *minerals* in sufficient quantities also are necessary. (Emphasis mine.)

We have briefly covered temperature and photoperiod as factors to be considered in greenhouse gardening, and the subject of water and minerals will be discussed later in the section on hydroponics. At this point we want to examine the important role played by carbon dioxide in plant growth.

The Most Important Fertilizer

Almost everyone knows that the gas that we breathe in is called oxygen (O^2), and it is essential to all life. What many people may not know, or have forgotten, is that the gas we breathe out is called carbon dioxide (CO^2), and it is no less essential to all life, since it is a vital ingredient used by plants in photosynthesis. Animal forms, from bacteria to man produce carbon dioxide through the process of respiration. (It is also produced in other ways, but for the purposes of the eco-system greenhouse we are primarily interested in carbon dioxide as a product of the respiration of higher animals and of the micro-organisms which produce compost.)

The normal concentration of carbon dioxide in the atmosphere is about three-hundred parts per million, yet from this seemingly meager supply, plants are able to grow and carry on all their vital functions. One explanation for the tremendous explosion of plant growth in the Coal Age is that the earth's atmosphere during that period contained more carbon dioxide than it does now. Plants grew faster than they were consumed, and the result was the creation of our present supply of coal, oil and gas — the so-called fossil fuels that we are now running out of.

Just as the electro-chemical energy manifested in your brain cells as you read these words was recently solar energy fixed by the process of photosynthesis in plants, so is the energy that powers your automobile as you drive to the corner store for a pack of cigarettes a manifestation of sunlight that was beamed to earth about two hundred and fifty million years ago. The fact that increased levels of carbon dioxide in the atmosphere produced such an abundance of plant growth during the days of the dinosaurs gives us an important clue as to how we can increase the yield of our greenhouse crops today.

Wittwer and Honma, in *Greenhouse Tomatoes — Guidelines for Successful Production*, tell us that:

> *Carbon dioxide has produced the most spectacular yield increases of any growth factor yet discovered in the culture of greenhouse crops.* ...Under some conditions, the most limiting factor in the growth of terrestrial plants is the carbon dioxide concentration in the atmosphere. This is particularly true for greenhouse crops since the carbon dioxide level in the enclosed atmosphere is often depleted far below that of the three-hundred parts per million in the outside air ...The increases in fruit yields range from ten to seventy percent, with averages of from fifteen to fifty-five percent. ...The response to carbon dioxide occurs over a wide range of light intensities. *It is possible to compensate partially for low light intensities such as occur on cloudy days by adding carbon dioxide to the atmosphere.* (Emphasis mine)

Everyone knows that plants must have fertilizer. Traditionally fertilizer has been thought of as organic matter or chemical salts which are applied directly to the soil. Not many growers think in terms of increasing the fertilizer content of the *atmosphere* in which the plants grow, despite the fact that it has been known for some time that *carbon dioxide is probably the most important single chemical ingredient needed by the plant.* In outdoor gardens it is impractical to think in terms of increasing the normal concentration of carbon dioxide in the air — how would one keep it from dispersing? In greenhouses, however, the grower can control the atmosphere. One aspect of proper ventilation, in addition to its cooling function, is that it allows fresh carbon dioxide to enter the greenhouse, thus replacing that which the plants have consumed. One reason that greenhouse crops don't do well in the wintertime, in addition to low temperatures and an inadequate photoperiod, is that, with the vents closed to conserve heat, the carbon dioxide is rapidly depleted to levels far below that of the outside air.

> **The air contains only about 300 parts per million of carbon dioxide. Thus vast volumes of air must be worked over by plants in order to obtain enough carbon in the form of carbon dioxide. In fact, if the air were richer in this substance, plants could grow faster and bigger than they do now.**
>
> **— *Hunger Signs in Crops*,**
> **National Fertilizer Association, 1949**

Michael Saxton of Harvard University, the man who first informed me of this important subject states that:

To some extent, extra carbon dioxide can make up for lack of light. An experiment with cucumbers shows this:

Full sunlight . . . . 100% yield

60% shade . . . . .64% yield

60% shade + CO_2 . . . . .92% yield

Full sunlight + CO_2 . . . . .147% yield

The added carbon dioxide is almost enough to make up for the 60% shade.

Commercial growers increase the carbon dioxide levels of their forcing structures to one-thousand to two-thousand parts per million. This is commonly accomplished by burning a natural gas such as propane for heating. (The products of combustion from this fuel are ideally a mixture of carbon dioxide and water vapor.)

Rabbits

Figure 7-1

Rabbits under hydroponic tanks in my original pit greenhouse.

I have increased the CO_2 level in my pit greenhouse to an estimated seven-hundred to eight-hundred parts per million by keeping rabbits in cages under the hydroponic tanks. An adult rabbit (the common Californian or New Zealand white variety) will produce about forty grams of carbon dioxide per day. In addition to these products of respiration, the composting rabbit manure, kept in bins, provides a certain amount of CO^2 as well as nitrogen in the form of ammonia gas. This latter is also utilized by the plants, since it has been estimated that a plant can get as much as ten percent of its nitrogen requirements from the air. Earthworms, which are raised in the manure bins, also produce CO^2, as well as the rich castings which can be utilized as an ingredient in the organic hydroponic solution to be described later. (See Figure 7-1.)

It is difficult to estimate the increase in crop yield from this technique, since I didn't have another greenhouse to use as a control when I performed these experiments. Suffice it to say that the plants exposed to increased CO^2 levels by the above methods *seemed* larger, healthier, and bore more and bigger fruit (tomatoes) than they did before the rabbits were added to the greenhouse. I have two color transparencies — one of the greenhouse taken in July of 1974, and one taken in July, 1975; the crops both seasons were the same, yet the plants photographed in 1975 were larger and more luxuriant than those photographed the previous year. Under the circumstances, this loose evidence hardly constitutes "scientific proof," but it is my opinion that the enrichment of the greenhouse atmosphere with the carbon dioxide of "rabbit breath" made the difference.

I have read the opinion of a rabbit breeder, apparently in response to the first edition of this book, that a greenhouse atmosphere is far too hot for rabbits. This certainly sounds plausible, but in my own experience the animals never exhibited any signs of stress. Their cages were on the floor of a pit greenhouse (where the air is coolest) and were never exposed to direct sunlight because of the shade of the hydroponic tanks. In warm weather the door and vents were open most of the time, providing continuous air circulation. Nevertheless, if experience shows that high temperatures are causing stress to the animals, it is certainly more humane to keep them inside only during the cool season when the closed greenhouse is most in need of the CO_2 they produce.

Rabbit Management

In addition to providing an enriched carbon dioxide supply to the greenhouse, intensive rabbit culture can result in significant yields of inexpensive protein. I kept four adult rabbits in the greenhouse — one buck and three does. The gestation period of a female rabbit is a convenient thirty days, and the rabbits are bred on a rotating schedule on the first day of every month.

To illustrate: On January first, rabbit A is bred. On February first, rabbit B is bred, and rabbit A is giving birth to an average of seven offspring. On March first, rabbit C is bred, rabbit B is giving birth, and rabbit A's litter is one month old. (Rabbit A could actually be bred again at this time, but I prefer not to work the creatures quite that much.) On April first, rabbit A is bred again, her litter is now two months old and ready for slaughter; rabbit C is kindling, and rabbit B's litter is one month old. The cycle is continued — once under way, on the first of the month you are always breeding a rabbit, a litter is being born, and a litter is ready for slaughter. In this way, if we assume an average of seven offspring per kindling, each female producing four litters a year, and all offspring harvested at a weight of five pounds, we can ideally come up with about 420 pounds of protein per year, or 105 pounds of protein per person for a family of four. This compares favorably with the production one might attain by raising a beef calf each year, but is much less expensive.

In order to get this kind of production from a herd of four rabbits, however, one must have the very best stock. Despite the mythology to the contrary, I have not found that rabbits are all that easy to raise. Some does only produce three or four in a litter, some allow their litters to die. For a while I had a buck that produced almost one-hundred percent male offspring. (The male sperm, not the female egg, determines the sex of the progeny.) This is not a problem if one is primarily interested in meat production for the table, but it does not allow one to improve the herd by careful selection of new females. It goes without saying that with good animals, and a program of constantly improving the herd, the above production figures might actually be improved.

At the time of this project only a comparatively small percentage of the greenhouse crops was fed to the rabbits. Often the lettuce grew faster than we could eat it, and the excess was given to them, but the bulk of their diet consisted of commercial rabbit pellets. It is not possible to feed these animals, plus their numerous progeny, from the greenhouse itself — not and have much food left for yourself! Nevertheless, the carbon dioxide and manure they produce, not to mention their protein, make rabbits a very important addition to the greenhouse.

Of course, if one has an attached greenhouse it is not desirable to keep animals and compost, along with their accumulated odors, in such close proximity to a habitation for people. The CO^2 produced by the humans in your dwelling will probably exceed that produced by rabbits, so in terms of carbon dioxide production, you're still ahead of the game.

An Experiment With Carbonated Water

A concentrated form of carbon dioxide is easily accessible in carbonated water or Club Soda. This is a common ingredient in mixed drinks and may be purchased from most supermarkets in both quart and liter bottles. Club Soda is just carbon dioxide (a gas) which has been combined with ordinary water (a liquid). The fizz you hear coming from your scotch and soda or can of soda pop is the sound of carbon dioxide dissipating into the atmosphere.

Because I grow my plants in hydroponic gravel beds which are flushed periodically with nutrient solution, I reasoned that I should be able to increase crop production by supplementing the hydroponic fluid with carbonated water; the escaping CO_2 gas would ideally be absorbed by both the roots and the leaves.

To test this theory, I planted two gravel-filled aluminum trays with lettuce and Chinese Cabbage seedlings. The first (control) tray received a normal flush of nutrient solution twice a day. In addition to the normal hydroponic solution, the second (experimental) tray was flushed with one quart of Club Soda at noon every other day. (The CO_2 must be provided when photosynthesis is near peak efficiency, or else the plant won't be able to use it.) The fluid was quickly removed from the tray as soon as the fizzing of the CO_2 gas subsided. The plant roots were then flushed with plain water. (This was necessary because of anticipated problems with the pH of Club Soda, which is not within the range of plant requirements. Despite my concern that I might be creating imbalances, I could detect no pH trauma to the plants.)

The results of the experiment were nothing short of astounding. Within a week the differences in plant growth between the two trays were clearly visible — within two weeks the plants receiving carbon dioxide were twice the size of the normal plants. This experiment was made sometime in 1978 or 1979, and I have unfortunately since lost my notes. If memory serves me correctly, however, the gross weight of the harvested CO_2 plants was significantly more than *double* that of the control plants. (See Figure 7-2.)

Figure 7-2

Control tray on left, and CO² tray on right, showing how carbonated water can increase hydroponic plant growth.

The reason I didn't continue with these experiments is the obvious one of the cost of Club Soda — at something like eighty cents a quart, this soon becomes a very expensive fertilizer. At the time of the experiment I intended to explore the use of a carbonator pump — a device used by bars and restaurants to manufacture their own Club Soda. Limited finances prevented me from following up on this, though it might prove to be a relatively inexpensive way to literally double crop production in a small hydroponic greenhouse. (The technique would probably not work on soil because of problems in draining the liquid after the CO_2 has been released, and the consequent pH predicament).

My "Club Soda" experiment lasted only a few weeks, and I have not repeated it, so I can't definitely state that it is a universally viable or practical technique. The initial results suggest that it is something well worth further investigation.

Update — 1991

As mentioned in the last chapter, the latest, state-of-the-art techniques of photoperiod control and carbon dioxide implementation have been developed by indoor marijuana growers. The reference cited there gives several methods for enriching a growing area with CO_2. One way which fits within the low-tech philosophy of this book would be to have several continuous batches of home brew percolating in the greenhouse: a by-product of fermentation is carbon dioxide.

To test this idea out, I began brewing a five-gallon batch of beer in my greenhouse in early September, 1991. It didn't take long to comprehend that in order to feed only a few potted tomato plants, I was attempting to saturate almost a thousand cubic feet of space with only one five-gallon crock of fermenting liquid. This seemed grossly inefficient, to say the least! Every little bit helps, of course, but in order to create really large amounts of CO_2 I'd have to turn the greenhouse into a veritable brewery.

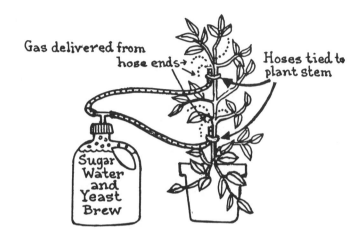

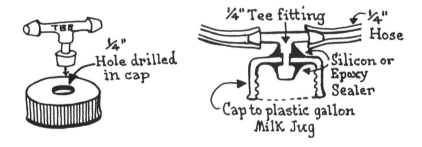

Figure 7-3

Construction and operation of a "home brewing" system that delivers carbon dioxide to individual plants..

In order to put the gas directly where it was needed, I constructed an individual plant feeder out of a plastic gallon milk jug. It took only a few minutes to drill a hole in the plastic cap and attach a drip irrigation "tee" fitting and two ¼-inch hoses. The fitting was secured to the cap with silicone sealer to prevent leakage. (See Figure 7-3.) Next, two cups of sugar were blended in the jug with a gallon of tepid water and a package of yeast. (At this point I wasn't as interested in creating drinkable brew as in making carbon dioxide.) The loose ends of each hose were then tied to the plant stem with wire twist fasteners, and in an hour or so the sugar-water-yeast mixture began to bubble. The carbon dioxide thus produced was piped directly to the plant via the hoses.

I observed this process for two days, then became curious about how well my test plant would respond to carbonated water being fed to it the same way. Consequently, I purchased five liters of Club Soda and each morning hooked up one of them to the plant by the same method. That is, in addition to the jug of fermenting sugar water, a Club Soda bottle equipped with a similar tee fitting and hoses was also tied to the plant every day for five days. Each container, no longer air-tight, gradually released its CO^2 through the feeding tubes. In this fashion it takes several hours for the soda to go completely flat — the same as if you left a bottle of Coca Cola open all day: by evening, there'd be no fizz left to it.

The test plant grew seven and a half inches in seven days, only five of which were supplemented with Club Soda. It was a quickie "experiment," and no control plants were measured, so these results hardly qualify as hard scientific data. Nevertheless, the technique appears worthy of repetition and further refinement.

Although the cost of Club Soda prohibits its use for any but plants of the highest value, the "fermentation bottle" is economical and could easily be adapted as a multiple plant feeder. For example, a five gallon spring water bottle full of home-brew and fitted with an air-tight cap could have a hose attached to an aquarium manifold; these are designed to supply several fish tanks with air from one pump, but in this case would supply several plants with carbon dioxide.

Of course, a fresh brew mixture must be started every week or so when the old one is ready to bottle. A beermaker's hydrometer, available from any store selling home-brew supplies, tells you when each batch is ready. If you're not interested in making beer, plain sugar water plus yeast will suffice. One pound of sugar per gallon of water is a good formula to start with. It's time to replace the mixture when the bubbles begin slowing down — usually in about a week, depending upon the ambient temperature in your greenhouse. The warmer the temperature, of course, the faster the yeast will work.

8

Hydroponics

Most publications on greenhouse tomato production sug-gest space allowances of 3 to 4 square feet per plant under soil culture. This is a population of 14,520 or 10,890 plants per acre, respectively. Plantings as dense as 18,500 per acre (about 2 square feet per plant) have been used in hydro-ponic culture in California and Arizona with good yields and quality.
— H.M. Resh, *Hydroponic Food Production*

Macronutrients

In addition to adequate levels of light and temperature, there are sixteen chemical elements required for the normal photosynthetic functioning of green plants. Carbon, hydrogen and oxygen are usually obtained from the air and water. (It is the mixture of carbon and oxygen that makes carbon dioxide.) Of the thirteen others, the big three, nitrogen (N), phosphorus (P) and potassium (K) are those required in the greatest quantity. Because of this, they are listed among the "macronutrients," and the percentages of N, P and K are what those three numbers on fertilizer containers refer to. The 7-6-19 printed on a box of *Hyponex*, for example, means that the chemical mixture contains seven percent nitrogen, six percent phosphorus, and nineteen percent potassium, or as it is sometimes also called, potash. The other macronutrients are calcium, magnesium and sulfur. They all normally enter the plant through its roots.

Micronutrients

The seven "micronutrients," so called because they are required in much less concentration, are no less important to plant growth. If the plant does not receive its needed amount of boron, for example, it will never grow normally, and will eventually die, even though the necessary quantity of the nutrient may be only a few parts per million. The same holds for the other micronutrients which are: chlorine, copper, iron, manganese, molybdenum and zinc.

Organic vs. Chemical Fertilizers

Plants in nature obtain these essential nutrients from the soil — manure, compost, and organic matter in general being the main sources. Microorganisms (soil bacteria) break down these organic materials and make the nutrients available to the plant in an inorganic form, i.e., *in the form of the chemical element concerned.* What this means is that nitrogen is nitrogen, whether it comes from compost or a chemical factory. The principal difference between chemical and organic fertilizers is essentially that the chemical fertilizer is already in the form that the plant can use immediately — no bacteria are needed to break it down first. Chemical fertilizers therefore act more quickly, though the essential nutrients are no different than those released by soil bacteria from organic sources. From the plant's point of view, the difference between the two methods — chemical vs. organic — is similar to the difference between medicine administered by intravenous injection and that given by a time-release capsule. Both medicines are identical: the difference to the plant lies in the method of administration and the speed at which it is able to absorb it.

The differences to the eco-system of which the garden is a part, however, are much more profound. If chemical fertilizers are continuously administered without any addition of organic material (a common agribusiness practice), the soil bacteria will eventually die, since there is no more organic matter for them to eat. The ultimate consequence is soil that is "dead"— nothing will grow on it unless chemical fertilizers are applied. For this reason alone, *the use of chemical fertilizers on soil is bad agriculture* — despite the fact that it is now the overwhelmingly prevalent method of crop husbandry in the world today.

Chemical agricultural practices, in conjunction with an interlocking web of other technological advances, have made possible an over-populated, urbanized world. The much slower, more natural pace of the organic method does not lend itself to the speeded-up efficiency of mechanization. The only way that China could feed six people from one acre of land in 1907 was because at least four of them were out there continuously cultivating that acre by hand. Like an addict who cannot live without drugs, the world has become so dependent upon chemical fertilizers that it is difficult to imagine any pathway back to a saner agricultural ecology short of mass starvation and all of the sociopolitical upheaval that goes with it. The fact that some chemical fertilizers are derived from our rapidly dwindling supplies of petroleum only exacerbates an already dangerous situation.

For these reasons, I would never put chemical fertilizers on my soil. However, unlike many organic gardening advocates, I have no objection, *per se,* to plants grown with "chemicals," since, all things being equal there can be absolutely no nutritional differences between vegetables grown by either method. Remember — nitrogen is nitrogen and phosphorus is phosphorus, whether it comes from composted rabbit manure or a test tube. *As far as the plant is concerned there can be no distinction between two atoms of the same chemical element.*

Many organic gardeners exude an air of pious dogmatism about this subject, as if there were something metaphysical about a phenomenon as natural as the sun rising and setting, or the cyclic procession of the seasons. Simultaneously they often exhibit a Luddite antipathy to all things "chemical" or "scientific." A report in the March 11, 1974 issue of *Newsweek* on the annual meeting of the American Association for the Advancement of Science puts the issue of plant nutrition into a more realistic perspective:

> The organic nutritionists' basic error is their assertion that organically grown foods are more nutritious than others because they receive all their nutrients from "natural" rather than synthetic inorganic sources. "A basic fact of plant nutrition is that plant roots absorb the nutrient elements from the soil only in an inorganic form," explained plant physiologist Daniel I. Arnon of the University of California. "Plant nutrients in organic manures and composts become available to plants only after they are converted into inorganic form by the activity of soil microorganisms."

> The experts at San Francisco were at pains to point out that they were not disparaging so-called natural foods... that is, products free of additives, preservatives, artificial

coloring and other chemicals added after the food has been harvested. "The health-food advocates may be on legitimate ground when they attack a number of additives found in foods," conceded Allentown, Pennsylvania psychiatrist Stephen Barret, a prime critic of the organic-growth industry. "However, they tend to lump together arguments for organic gardening and against food additives as though one is naturally linked to the other — when, in fact, they are entirely different issues."

To give some perspective to this issue it must also be acknowledged that chemical fertilizer adherents often exhibit the same uncritical enthusiasm for their own particular beliefs. Proselytizers for hydroponics (usually, but not always, a "pure chemical" method) are often guilty of this. The following quotation from *Hydroponic Gardening* by R. Bridwell is just one example: "The superior nutritive value of hydroponic produce has definitely been established by laboratory analysis."

Considering the data presented above, how could such a claim possibly be accurate? We live in a culture long-accustomed to the hyperbole of advertising and perhaps have learned to believe in our own enthusiasms far past the frontiers of literal truth. Hydroponic greenhouse gardening has many advantages which will be explained below, but the value and usefulness of the technique does not depend upon claims which contradict proven facts.

Hydroponics

The American Heritage Dictionary of the English Language defines "hydroponics" as follows:

hy-dro-pon-ics (hi'dre-pon'iks) *n.* Plural in form, used with a singular verb. The cultivation of plants in water containing dissolved inorganic nutrients, rather than in soil.

I have been growing hydroponic greenhouse vegetables for over sixteen years now, and I am convinced that (when properly understood and carried out) hydroponics is the quickest and simplest method for gaining the maximum amount of produce from a minimum amount of growing area. It is this fact which makes hydroponics ideally suited to the space restrictions encountered in the average small home greenhouse.

Advantages of the Hydroponic Method

The point is important enough to bear repeating: *The greatest advantage of the hydroponic method is that crop yields are increased many times over those of conventional agriculture.* For example, the yield of tomatoes grown in soil is from five to ten tons per acre; with hydroponics, the harvest is boosted to *between sixty and three-hundred tons per acre!*

For cucumbers, the equivalent per acre statistics are: three-and-a-half tons in soil, compared with *fourteen tons* for hydroponics — for lettuce, four-and-a-half tons, soil, versus *ten-and-a-half tons*, hydroponics.

In addition, it is estimated that hydroponic methods require only one-twentieth to one-thirtieth the amount of water required by conventional soil gardening, thus making it possible to grow large amounts of food in arid and semi-arid environments. This is because the solution is captured and saved to be recycled over and over again. The only losses come from evaporation and the amount of liquid which is actually absorbed by the plants. Of course, the solution must be monitored and regularly supplemented with both water and nutrients as required.

Another advantage is that hydroponics lends itself to automation — a very important fact for people who can't always be around when their plants need attention. It is even possible to go away for several days without having to worry about the plants' survival. The technology for this is very simple, and uses an insignificant amount of electrical energy.

Because my interests in food production are focused on getting the maximum efficient yield from the least amount of space and energy input, almost all of the vegetables in my greenhouses are raised by this method.

Hydroponics was originally developed as a scientific methodology to determine the nutrients essential to plant life. In order to isolate these nutrients, plants were raised without soil, receiving instead solutions of various dissolved chemical salts. By means of this technique, most of the sixteen chemical nutrients previously described were determined. From these discoveries evolved the era of chemical fertilizers and a fundamental misunderstanding of plant nutrition by overly enthusiastic advocates of both organic and chemical agriculture.

Basic to the organic method is the adage: "feed the soil, not the plant." The rationale being that with enough organic material in the soil, the plant will automatically receive an adequate balance of nutrients. The point of view of chemical agriculture, however, is just the opposite: "feed the plant, you can't eat the dirt." Obviously, *when raising crops in the conventional manner, in soil, the organic method is the only ecologically sane technique*, for all of the reasons previously mentioned.

When raising plants in hydroponic culture, however, one *must* feed the plant, since the sand or gravel used as a supporting medium for the roots is completely inert, containing no nutrients at all. It is this aspect of hydroponics — the ability to feed the plant all of its essential nutrients in proper balance, in a form which makes them instantly available (plants "drink" their food, they can't "eat" it), and without "poisoning" anything more valuable than a few cubic feet of gravel — which makes it outproduce vegetables grown in soil three to one, or more. Because the plant receives its food in a liquid form, it doesn't have to expend energy in developing a huge root system. Instead, it puts most of its growth into foliage and fruit — thus increasing the yield.

Plants growing in soil must develop large root systems as they seek out the nutrients necessary to their survival. In addition they are dependent upon the soil bacteria to break down organic matter into the necessary chemical elements. Hydroponics short-circuits all this — the plant's food is *brought* to it in a liquid form which is immediately utilized.

In India, it has been estimated that one acre of hydroponic garden is capable of continuously supplying 1,800 people with three pounds of vegetable food each day. Since I have never heard of this being done in reality, we must take such claims with a grain of salt. (Actually, I hope that the claim is the gross exaggeration it appears to be, since the last thing the world needs is the population density that such agriculture would make possible.) Suffice it to say that hydroponic gardening has the capability of providing tremendous yields of vegetable crops — much more so than is easily practical with conventional soil cultivation.

It has sometimes been suggested that the extensive use of hydroponic greenhouses, with their greater yields of produce, could actually *free* our cropland for organic agriculture. Bear in mind that the earth is already unable to feed its continuously booming population. That's the main reason why chemical fertilizers must be used: natural methods can no longer keep up with our terrifying clamor for nourishment. As we all know, the situation is serious, and deteriorating rapidly — at the time of this writing, there are more than five billion human stomachs to fill each day on this planet. (Never mind that most of them *aren't* being filled!) Doesn't it make some sense to solve at least a part of the problem with hydroponic methods rather than poison our cropland beyond the point of easy recovery? Even if petro-chemical hydroponic solutions were applied, it would still be a much better use of our dwindling petroleum supplies than burning them up in freeway commuter cars.

At this point it should be emphasized that the tremendous yields from the hydroponic method are not miracles. It is *theoretically* possible to get the same results from soil culture, but in practice it seldom works out that way. Because the chemical makeup of hydroponic solutions is easier to formulate and control, it gains a big edge over more conventional growing methods. There are many variables in soil culture which are not easily controlled — how much water, and when to apply it? What is the exact chemical composition of the organic matter in the soil, and are the soil bacteria making the nutrients available in enough quantity for maximum growth? In hydroponic culture the water and the nutrients are both applied at the same time, and each solution can be adjusted to meet the nutrient requirements of the specific plant under cultivation — a tremendous advantage when growing several species simultaneously in separate tanks.

Plants, like animals, have differing nutritional requirements; just as a diet adequate for a sheep would starve a pig, so a balance of nutrients adequate for grapes probably wouldn't produce very many healthy tomatoes.

Generally speaking, hydroponic gardening requires that the grower learn a little more about plant physiology and nutrient requirements than the average soil gardener. This is neither difficult nor particularly time-consuming. In a very real sense, using the hydroponic method in a home greenhouse can be a consciousness expanding activity — a kind of "plant yoga."

Sub-irrigation

Most plants grown hydroponically are raised in greenhouses under carefully controlled conditions. Pea gravel or perlite is usually used as a medium for root support, and a balanced liquid mixture of all the necessary nutrients is periodically fed to the plants from below. This method is called "sub-irrigation culture." In large commercial greenhouses the technique has been refined to such a degree, that once the seedlings have been planted, almost all the work is done by automation. Delicate sensors in the growing medium decide when the plants need more solution and switch on pumps which meter out the correct dosage.

Manual Systems

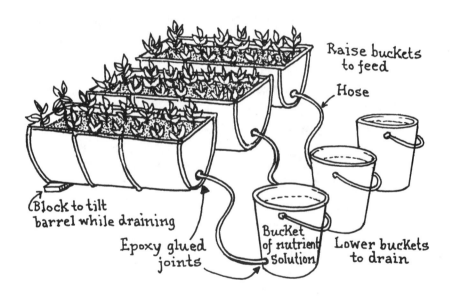

Figure 8-1

Schematic of a manual hydroponic system. The five gallon drums are lifted at feeding time until empty, then are placed on the floor again where the solution flows back into them.

Figure 8-2

The author using a manual system to irrigate vegetables in a hydroponic greenhouse.

My original greenhouse was much less energy-intensive than this. Although I no longer use this kind of manual system, it is a classic design which is still useful under many circumstances. Here is how it is constructed:

The hydroponic tanks consist of several fifty-five gallon drums cut in half lengthwise — each drum dividing into two tanks. At the bottom of every trough is brazed a three inch length of one-half inch O.D. copper tubing. A four foot length of one-half inch I.D. garden hose is then clamped to this tube, and the other end similarly attached to another tube brazed on the bottom of a five gallon can. The insides of both the tank and the can are painted with a thick coating of asphalt-based paint. This is to prevent the metal surfaces from rusting, since they are obviously constantly exposed to moisture. To prevent pebbles from clogging the hose, it is essential that a small piece of fiberglass screen be placed over the tube inside the trough before gravel is installed. The drum half is then filled to within a few inches of the top with pea-sized gravel.

In using a system like this, the five-gallon can is filled with the hydroponic solution. When it is time to feed the plants, this container is lifted so that it is higher than the growing tank. The fluid runs down the hose and into the gravel, irrigating the plant roots from below. As soon as the container is empty, it is returned to the floor and the liquid drains from the gravel, down the hose and back into the can. In summer this should be done at least three times a day — morning, noon and evening — so that the roots of the crops are always kept moist. (See Figure 8-2.)

A Superior Tank

Since those early experiments, I've discovered that a much better hydroponic tank can be made from a defunct electric water heater. These can be found fairly often in almost any dump; or ask your local plumber to save some for you. (The more common gas water heaters aren't as useful because they have a vent-pipe running up their centers, which gets in the way of growing space.) The tank is cut in half lengthwise with a metal-cutting power saw or oxy-acetylene torch; it is divided so that the drain fitting is at the bottom of the trough, where a PVC street elbow and short length of pipe with a faucet is installed. (Don't forget to put a piece of fiberglass screen over the inside drain hole to prevent gravel from clogging the pipe and faucet.) Because most water heaters have a porcelainized interior they will not rust, and therefore need no asphalt-based paint. This, plus the fact that they are made of heavier gauge steel, is what makes them superior to the 55-gallon drum tanks.

Figure 8-3

Hydroponic tank made from half of an electric water heater. Note the faucet for draining the tank at lower right.

It is a simple matter to manually pour the hydroponic solution into the gravel-filled tank (faucet closed), replace the nutrient receptacle under the faucet, and then open the valve to drain the tank. I've found this method to be the quickest and easiest of the manual systems, though one has to be careful not to pour the solution so fast that it churns up the gravel around the plant roots. (See Figure 8-3.)

A Modest Experiment

Hydroponic growing is so easy, productive and efficient that one doesn't even need a greenhouse to utilize its advantages. As a controlled experiment one winter I planted four 11 x 19-inch aluminum-foil roaster pans (the "throw-away" type used for Thanksgiving turkeys) with lettuce and Chinese Cabbage seeds and placed them in my bedroom window. (The only modification necessary was to epoxy a short length of plastic tubing to the pan bottoms for drainage — a mini-version of the systems described above.) These four hydroponic "tanks" had a combined surface area of 5.1 square feet, which is roughly four square feet *smaller* than the top of an average-sized card table. Although the window, which faced seventy-five degrees east of due south, was not the best orientation for growing anything, it was at that time the only natural light source available, so I used it.

The seeds were planted on December 18th. I began trimming lettuce and cabbage leaves on February 19th, and continued that harvest on a daily basis from all four trays until March 19th. During the timed one-month interval of this experiment, I trimmed a total of 6.15 pounds of greens from the 5.1 square-foot hydroponic garden. That works out to about 1.2 pounds of edible tissue per square foot of growing space per month. Put in more immediate terms, it means that I was able to eat a fresh green salad every night for a month in late winter, and that all of those salads were harvested from a space only slightly larger than half the top of a card table! (See Figure 8-4.)

This is why I like the hydroponic method. If you could maintain this level of production for a full year, you'd find your-self raising over 14 pounds of food for every square foot of growing space. That figures out to around 70 pounds of leafy green vegetables from only 5.1 square feet of hydroponic window box. If you grew only lettuce, which currently averages about eighty cents per pound in the local supermarkets, you'd be shaving more than fifty dollars a year from your food bill.

Figure 8-4

Lettuce plants growing in hydroponic window box.

It's easy to wax enthusiastic about abstract figures like this, so I must hasten to add that it is not quite so easy to get production figures of this sort in November, December, January and early February. The section on "Effective Growing Season" (Chapter 2) explains why. Although supplementary heat, carbon dioxide and artificial lighting can make up the difference, one must add the energy costs of these measures to the total value of the crops produced to determine their feasibility.

Feeding Schedules

Plant nutrient requirements are intricately interrelated with temperature, photoperiod and the carbon dioxide supply. If the growth rate is slow due to a deficiency in any of these other factors (as in wintertime), then more nutrients will not make up the difference. During the winter a feeding schedule of once in three days might be all that is required, whereas in summer three times in one day could actually be insufficient. When using the manual systems described above, the grower must learn to quickly and instinctively respond to the plants' nutrient requirements: one error on a hot July afternoon could mean the demise of many valuable plants, not to mention the waste of all the hours and energy invested in growing them. That's a time-consuming cross to bear, and a strategy which usually turns out to be highly impractical. You may be forgiven if you have other things to do than constantly monitor the condition of the plants in your greenhouse.

Automated Systems

In addition, lifting five gallon cans (each one full of forty pounds of nutrient solution) three times a day may not be everyone's idea of pleasant exercise. For these reasons one soon learns to appreciate the value of automation in a hydroponic greenhouse. There are many methods of accomplishing this, few of which use much energy. I have either built or observed several such systems and have finally and enthusiastically settled on one which is so efficient, so elegant in design, that I won't even bother to describe the others.

The Nutrient Flow Technique (NFT)

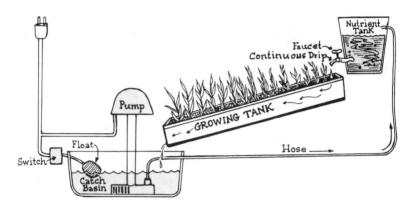

Figure 8-5

Schematic drawing of Nutrient Flow Technique.

Dr. P.A. Schippers, of the Long Island Horticultural Research Farm run by Cornell University, has developed a unique and highly efficient hydroponic growing system. Named the Nutrient Flow Technique, hereafter referred to as NFT, the method is almost foolproof in its simplicity, and offers greenhouse owners a way to grow large amounts of food in very small spaces. It is so automatic that one could go away for weeks at a time without worrying about plants in the greenhouse, and so energy efficient that I estimate it would take more than one year of continuous operation to use up one kilowatt hour of electricity. The system is flexible enough to serve the needs of large commercial greenhouses, or could be scaled down to work equally well as a windowsill unit in a city apartment. In addition to all of these advantages, the design can even be modified to take advantage of vertical space in the greenhouse — the back or north wall, for example — thus productively using areas not normally utilized for growing.

Figure 8-6

Growing trough made from 2 x 4 module with black vinyl plastic sheeting to create trough. (Photo courtesy Dr. P.A. Schippers, Cornell University.)

The method works on little more than gravity plus a float-switch and electric pump. A slow but continuous flow of nutrient solution drips from an elevated tank down a slightly inclined trough planted with vegetables. The solution is captured at the end of the trough in a holding tank or catch basin. When the solution in this latter container reaches a predetermined level, a float (identical to the type used in toilets) trips an electrical switch which turns on a small pump. The nutrient liquid is then pumped through a hose back to the elevated tank to be recycled again down the growing trough. When the level of fluid is depleted in the lower holding basin the float switch automatically turns the pump off. (See Figure 8-5.) The units which I built run about fifteen seconds every eight hours. At that rate, the energy consumption is so small as to not even show up on your electric bill, and is obviously highly compatible with the limitations inherent in alternative energy systems.

The NFT may easily be expanded to more than one growing trough. Dr. Schippers nails eight-foot lengths of 2″ x 4″ lumber to a standard sheet of 4′ x 8′ plywood, thus creating a thirty-two square foot growing module. The 2 x 4s are spaced about six inches apart (distance is not terribly critical). Over these 2 x 4s he lays a large sheet of 4 mil. black vinyl, pushing it down between them to create several plastic lined troughs. A manifold, made up of ordinary PVC pipe and the appropriate fittings, has a faucet or drip-irrigation outlet at each trough; a long catch basin at the opposite end of the module catches the run-off. A truly amazing amount of food can thus be produced from an area the size of a sheet of plywood — thirty-two square feet.

Figure 8-7

Lettuce seedlings in Jiffy-7s placed in trough. Note that there is no other root support. (Photo courtesy Dr. P.A. Schippers, Cornell Univesity.)

Figure 8-8

Wider view, showing seedlings planted in several growing modules. Note the nutrient container (garbage can) in aisle at right of photo. (Photo courtesy Dr. P.A. Schippers, Cornell University.)

Figure 8-9

Several weeks later, the lettuce is ready for harvest.
(Photo courtesy Dr. P.A. Schippers, Cornell University.)

Figure 8-10

The author's first NFT system. PVC grow beds drain into the bucket at right, where the solution is pumped back to the storage tank at the other end of the beds.

These troughs may be filled with perlite (gravel is too abrasive on the thin vinyl) and plants then spaced in them accordingly. In fact, a root-support medium isn't even necessary for some plants when using this system. Dr. Schippers starts lettuce seedlings in jiffy cubes without any further root supporting medium at all. The cubes are spaced down the troughs and the lettuce grows to maturity supported only by the cube, the sides of the trough, and its fellow plants.

Figure 8-11

Two sets of grow beds in the author's L-shaped attached greenhouse.

Figure 8-12

The author tends his tomatoes. While difficult to see in this black and white photo, the crop is ripe and red and ready to eat.

Obviously, modules of any convenient size can be created to suit individual situations. Because I didn't like the aesthetics of black vinyl sheeting, I created a unit composed of four-inch diameter PVC drain pipe with sections cut out to provide a trough. It is important to make them from a stable, inert material: galvanized rain-gutter, for instance, would be unsuitable because of the danger of too much zinc getting into the nutrient solution.

Figure 8-13

A close-up of the hydroponic grow beds. Note that plant roots are supported by only a few inches of gravel.

Utilizing Vertical Space with the NFT

The NFT concept described above can easily be modified to create a vertical growing space. Dr. Schippers has created what he calls "lettuce trees" by cutting many small square holes in one side of a section of one-and-a-half-inch diameter PVC pipe. The

Figure 8-14

The NFT system can utilize vertical space in a greenhouse. Seedlings are placed in the square holes cut into one-and-a-half or two-inch PVC pipe. Nutrient holding tank is elevated above the pipes, as seen in left rear of photo (on top of crates). (Photo courtesy of Dr. P.A. Schippers, Cornell University.)

length of the pipe can be as tall as you want your "tree" to be, and the holes should be just big enough to snugly accept one jiffy cube. Several such pipes are placed in a row vertically, and a

Figure 8-15

"Lettuce trees" at harvest stage — an elegant and ingenious use of vertical space in a greenhouse. (Photo courtesy Dr. P.A. Schippers, Cornell University.)

drip-irrigation hose is positioned above them with a drip fitting entering each pipe at the top. The pipes rest in a catchment trough fitted with a float switch and pump — operating on the same principle described earlier. The nutrient tank, of course, must be elevated high enough above the tops of the pipe-trees for the hydroponic fluid to flow into them via the drip-irrigation hose and fittings. Each jiffy cube with its lettuce seedling will remain moist from the continuous flow from above and will quickly grow into a large plant. (See Figures 8-14 and 8-15.)

Planting

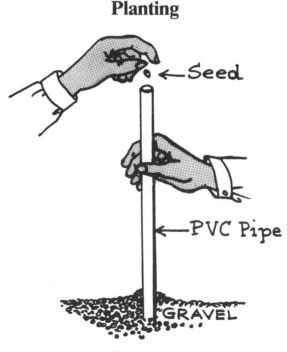

Figure 8-16

A simple seed planting tube.

The usual procedure for planting in gravel is to start seedlings in peat pots or jiffy cubes. Once the plants are well started it is a simple matter to place the entire unit in the gravel. Sometimes planting the seeds directly in the gravel is sufficient. One method is to use a short length of one-half inch diameter PVC pipe as a planting tube. (See Figure 8-16.) The bottom of the pipe is pushed into the gravel about a quarter of an inch, and the seed dropped into the top end, thus making it easy to space the plants as desired. This generally works best with the larger seeds — tiny seeds, such as carrots (which I don't recommend you grow hydroponically anyway), can be flushed through the gravel by the nutrient solution to finally sprout where you don't want them.

The Taste of Hydroponic Vegetables

One often hears the complaint that hydroponic vegetables (usually tomatoes) bought in supermarkets taste bland and pulpy. The explanation for this (aside from the fact that super-market produce is of dubious freshness) is that tomatoes grown in commercial hydroponic greenhouses are usually special hybrids, bred for color, uniformity of size, and the ability to ripen all at the same time — qualities which have nothing to do with flavor, but everything to do with the convenience and profit of the agribusinessman who raises them. No special hybrids for me — the tomatoes I raise are the same varieties I grow in the garden — Burpee Big Boy being a particular favorite.

Several years ago I conducted an informal test — two tomatoes, one from the garden, and the other from the green-house, were sliced and placed on separate plates. These were offered to a group of skeptical friends for analysis — "Which tomato was raised hydroponically?" No one could detect any difference, or correctly identify which tomato came from outside and which was grown in a tank.

Organic Hydroponics

About the only criticism of hydroponic growing that I will accept as valid is that it relies to a certain degree on chemicals which are derived from fossil fuels, or which burn fossil fuels in their manufacture.

Since the hydroponic method was originally developed as a scientific means of determining the mineral nutrients required by plants, it is not surprising that in its commercial applications it has traditionally relied on pure chemical salts for its solutions. Very little research seems to have been done with organically derived formulas. Perhaps the most notable work that has been undertaken along these lines was carried out in India. James S. Douglas, in his book, *Hydroponics: The Bengal System*, describes something known as the "Sharder process" which was developed at the Hydroponics and Fish Investigation Unit in Bengal:

> Normal beds of aggregate are employed for raising plants, but to supply essential nourishment to crops, manure shells or pots are placed at appropriate intervals along the trough. These consist of earthenware vessels, lined with some kind of sieve or screen, and pierced by a number of tiny holes at the bottoms. The pots are filled with a nutrient sludge or semi-liquid manure, a typical formula for which would be:
>
> > Fresh or dried dung, one handful
> > Matured oil cakes, four teaspoonfuls.
>
> Alternatively, such materials as hoof-and-bone meal, shoddy (wool waste), and similar plant foodstuffs can be utilized, the exact quantities depending upon their analyses. Dried wood ashes are also fairly good for the purpose...
>
> When the manure shells are placed in the hydroponic troughs, and sunk down a few inches into the aggregate,

with only the upper portions remaining exposed, they slowly release their nutrient contents into the growing medium. These then become available to the plant's roots as food. Covers should be placed over the vessels, and from time to time they may be refilled with nutrient sludge or topped up. Every three months the beds should be flushed through with plain water to cleanse them.

Fish Tank Nutrient Solution

Another experiment with an organic nutrient solution is briefly described on page 135 of *Energy Primer* (1974). This method uses the water from aquaculture tanks as a growth medium:

> Finally, associated with each main (fish) tank is a hydroponic growing compartment where the culture water from the main tanks (a "soup" of excellent fertilizer) is flushed through gravel beds planted with vegetable crops.

My initial feeling when I read this was that the fish tank water would probably not provide an adequate diet of nutrients for optimum growth. Consequently, to test this, I started some hydroponic pinto beans, using only the water from the aquaculture tank as a culture medium. At first, these plants put on amazing growth — rising several inches above their contemporaries growing in a commercial solution. Then, after a couple of weeks, the commercial beans began to catch up with those receiving only fish tank water. By the end of the month, the fish tank beans had all but stopped growing and were pale and sickly in appearance, while the other beans were in all respects normal.

These results seem to be at least partially confirmed by an experiment conducted at the U.S. Fish and Wildlife Service's fish farming experiment station in Stuttgart, Arkansas. In the May/June 1975 issue of *Aquaculture and the Fish Farmer*,

Sneed, Allen and Ellis report on the experiment, which involved flushing the effluent from a raceway complex containing ten-thousand pounds of Channel Catfish into hydroponic troughs containing seventeen varieties of vegetables. In general, the results of the experiment were disappointing:

> The yield of edible tissue varied widely among different vegetable varieties. Although (all) varieties produced some edible tissue, eleven were of very poor quality and quantity. Three varieties produced average yields and three produced yields considered to be above average for home gardens. The best yields were produced by green peas and cucumbers.

In most cases, then, people who are combining aquaculture with hydroponics should consider using the fish tank water as an excellent starter — a basic solution with which to mix other organic materials.

Lawrence D. Weiss, in the May 14, 1973 issue of *The Tribal Messenger*, gives us a clue as to how to mix an organic hydroponic solution:

> Once the location of the hydroponic installation has been determined, and the troughs built, the hard work is done with. The last major concern is the nutrient solution itself. Home-made mixtures of such things as well-rotted compost and animal manure are cheap and ecological. The home farmer can experiment with different such nutrients and strengths in the water base. In this way he or she will find the combination most suitable for his or her plants and installation.

Using both fish tank and well water as base liquids, I mixed several different strengths, mixes and types of organic material — in effect, creating what is familiar to most organic gardeners as "manure tea." I used these solutions on tomatos, radishes, lettuce, runner and pinto beans. Most of the initial experiments were with beans. At the same time, identical plants received the commercial hydroponic solution (*Hyponex*: 7-6-19).

The Organic Mix

At first I was very "scientific" — carefully weighing out twenty grams of rabbit manure per liter of water, for example. I soon realized that such careful measurements were unnecessary, and that in any case few home growers would bother to be so exacting. In my experience it didn't seem to matter at all, and I wound up mixing a standard formula consisting of:

> One part rabbit manure;
> One part chicken manure;
> One part earthworm castings;
> One part wood ashes.

The measure used was a small *Quaker Oats* box, filled to the top. The only convenient container I had for mixing these ingredients was a twenty gallon can, which was filled to within an inch or so of the top with either well or fish tank water. (I can't honestly say that I noticed much difference between the two, though it stands to reason that the fish tank liquid would have more nutrients in it.) Rain water should probably not be used, however, since it is presumably deficient in the micronutrients (manganese, boron, etc.) which are usually always present as impurities in ground water.

The organic ingredients were vigorously stirred into the water and then allowed to steep for several days, by which time all solid particles had settled to the bottom. The liquid (the color of a weak cup of tea) was then carefully poured off into cans and fresh water added to the container for a new batch. I found that I could get several batches of hydroponic fluid from one batch of organic material. From time to time I would add fresh measures of the organic mix to the liquid — relying mostly on my intuition when it was time to do so.

Testing the pH

At first, I very religiously tested the pH of all my solutions. pH is the measure of how acidic or alkaline a material is on a scale from 1 to 14. The lower the pH number, the more acid; the higher the pH number, the more alkaline, or basic. On a scale of 14 possible degrees, the number 7 is obviously the neutral, or balance point between the two extremes. Plants will only thrive within certain rather narrow pH ranges, and each plant species has its own unique requirements, some liking acid conditions, some alkaline or basic. Fortunately, most of the vegetables we are interested in raising will do well on a neutral to slightly acid pH.

All of the books on hydroponics really stress the importance of regular testing, but in my experience, the pH of my solutions, both organic and commercial, has almost always been right about where it should be — between 6.0 and 7.0. The middle of this range — pH 6.5 — is considered ideal for most garden vegetables. Because the point is always emphasized in the hydroponic literature, I must responsibly follow suit — pH is important, and should be checked at least once a week. Some sources say every four days. For some reason, I am lucky — I've just never had problems with it.

The pH test is made with a special litmus indicator tape. A common type, called *Nitrazine* paper, is available from any drug store. When a strip of this paper tape is dipped into the fluid to be tested it will change color depending on the pH — yellow for strongly acid, blue for strongly alkaline, with several ranges in between. The hue of the paper is then matched against a color chart on the side of the container it comes in. (For those who are unfamiliar with this very simple test, don't be alarmed — it really isn't complicated.)

If the solution turns out to be too alkaline, an acid must be added to bring it in line with the proper pH, or if too acid, an alkali or base must be added. Commercial hydroponic green-houses use, of course, pure hydrochloric acid or sodium hydroxide to balance the pH of their nutrient solutions. Since each of these chemicals is *extremely dangerous*, I have relied on white vinegar (acid) or baking soda (alkali-base) with no problems at all. A common rule of thumb states that one teaspoon of white distilled vinegar will lower the pH of one gallon of water by one point.

To someone who has no familiarity with simple chemistry, this may sound strange and possibly complex — it isn't, and no one should be put off from trying hydroponics because of it. Actually, I have seldom had to adjust the pH of my solutions — to the point where I ruefully admit to often neglecting to do the testing.

Yield From Organic Solution

The results of my experiments indicate that almost any organically-derived solution will grow plants. The bean plants raised in a pure chicken manure solution grew just as rapidly as those raised with the above described mixture. I must be honest and state that the control plants, raised in pure worm castings (no soil at all) grew as well as any of the hydroponic plants, including those receiving the commercial solution. In general, the commercial solution plants grew slightly faster than the organic solution plants, but not significantly so. (See Figure 8-17.) The most striking difference between the two solutions was that the organic plants usually did not wilt during the hottest part of the day, while the plants raised with the commercial solution almost always wilted. I observed this phenomenon take place every day, so it isn't a figment of my imagination.

Figure 8-17

Bean plants raised in organic hydroponic solution (left), fish tank water (middle), and Hyponex (right).

An excessively high nutrient salt concentration near the plant roots can cause a plant to lose water to the soil, or in this case, to the gravel. The result is wilting of the leaves. Since the commercial solution plants were probably receiving a higher concentration of nutrients than the organic solution plants, this provides a possible explanation for the wilting phenomenon. Bear in mind that the summer greenhouse temperatures, even with all vents open, sometimes go as high as one-hundred and four degrees F. — a temperature at which any self-respecting plant would wilt. Within five minutes of being flushed with solution, however, all symptoms disappeared — the same as when one waters wilting plants in the garden or in pots.

Since my organic hydroponic experiments were quite modest, I hesitate to make definitive statements about the method. Much research remains to be done. For those interested in experimenting with organic hydroponic solutions, *The Complete Book of Composting* (Rodale, 1971), lists the NPK percentages of most common organic materials. (For example, rabbit manure has NPK percentages of 7.0, 2.4, and 0.6) By composting appropriate mixtures of organic materials, then leaching them with water, hydroponic solutions of varying NPK percentages may be produced.

Apparently the other nutrients — both macro and micro — are usually present in sufficient quantities in the water or organic material to produce adequate growth. Using organic fluids I have never had any plant deficiency symptoms relating to minerals other than nitrogen. (The beans grown in the pure fish tank water were deficient in this element.)

Animal Feed

One technique you may wish to try is to raise "hydroponic" oats, barley, or rye grass as animal feed during the winter. Although technically considered a hydroponic procedure, this is essentially just the extended sprouting of seeds for animal, rather than human, consumption. The main difference is that here the sprouts are allowed to grow into small plants.

Cover the bottom of some shallow trays (throw-away aluminum pie tins are ideal) with a layer of barley (or other) seed to a depth of about half an inch. Having thus obtained the correct measure for your pans, transfer the seeds to a large jar. Run water into this container until the seeds are completely covered and place the jar in a warm, dark place without a lid for a couple of days. (It is not necessary to use a chemical solution — the water alone will suffice.) After about 48 hours, give the seeds a thorough rinsing and return them to the tray, keeping it covered with a moist cloth. Flush the seeds with fresh water twice a day to prevent them from drying out. (By the same token, do not let them permanently soak or they will begin to rot.) When the sprouted seeds have reached a height of about half an inch, remove the cloth and place the tray in a sunny window. At night it may be necessary to relocate them near a heat source to maintain them at a more or less constant room temperature. You will soon have a thick, tightly-woven mat of lush green "grass" that is an ideal winter fodder for chickens, rabbits or goats. By starting a new batch of seed every few days, one can maintain a continuous supply of winter forage that animals really love. (See Figures 8-18 and 8-19.)

Figure 8-18

*Three aluminum pans with various growth stages
of barley sprouts for winter animal feed.*

Figure 8-19

Chickens love my greenhouse sprouts.

The mat of grass grown in this way is so tightly compact, that it occurs to me that this might be a convenient way to grow your own sod for lawns. In such a case, of course, one would use regular grass seed rather than grains.

Update — 1991

Since I made those long-ago original investigations I've grown somewhat older, conceivably wiser, hopefully less self-righteous, and assuredly a lot lazier. It is less trouble to stir up a batch of commercial hydroponic solution than it is to put together an organic mixture, and I haven't bothered doing the latter for many years now. A normal batch of *Hyponex*, for example, is created from only one teaspoon of dry chemical to one gallon of water; the resulting solution will feed my plants every day for a *minimum* of one week (usually at least three times longer than that) — which is another way of saying that a very little goes a very long way. If I am thereby depleting the earth of its resources, it is at least arguable that I won't burn in hell too long for my share of the damages.

Access

Hydroponic Chemicals
Hyponex
Hydroponic Chemical Co.
Copley, OH 44321

Super-Gro
Hydroponics Co.
PO Box 3215
Little Rock, AR 72201

Continental Nutriculture Co.
Box 6751
Lubbock, TX 79409
(Manufactures a custom formula based upon the chemical content of local water supply and individual growing conditions.)

Dr. Chatelier's Plant Food
PO Box 20375
St. Petersburg, FL 33742

9

Greenhouse Management

For the kitchen, the greenhouse will bring in a longer harvest of your favorite vegetables. It can be managed like a storehouse of living food if the vegetables are planted to mature in late summer and picked into early winter.

— John White, "Crops for the Solar Greenhouse,"
The Solar Greenhouse Book

We have seen how the optimum photosynthetic functioning of green plants is dependent upon complex interrelationships of temperature, light, and carbon dioxide supply, and how the plant roots and stem act as a water system which transports the proper mixture of dissolved mineral nutrients to where they can complete their part of the process. If we are sensitive to the harmony of these interactions we will have constructed our greenhouse to provide for their fulfillment. As eco-system gardeners, we are a necessary link in this chain of relationships, for it is our management which keeps the process in motion. While we are providing for the plants, the plants are providing for us — in more ways than one, since the alteration of the grower's consciousness engendered by working with such a system is probably equally as important as the food it produces. If everyone had an eco-system greenhouse, I doubt if there would be an environmental crisis in the world today. It is one thing to read about ecological laws, it is quite another to experience their full reality in one's everyday life. If we accept the notion that the goal of all true religion is to unite the individual spirit with the larger reality of which it is a part, then the laws of ecology might fit that definition better than some ostensible religions, and a greenhouse, properly regarded and managed, might fulfill the role of a church better than many ostensible churches.

Sowing and Reaping

Proper management of the greenhouse eco-system is the key to maximum productivity. Like anything else, you reap pretty much what you sow, and if you want continuous reaping you must be prepared for continuous sowing. It is really as simple as that, and it is surprising how long it took me to discover a fact so obvious. Rule number one is:

Never allow a productive square inch to remain fallow.

Even if only a radish or two, always plant seeds just as soon as space is available for them. This will involve some judgement on your part, and often mean the ruthless termination of plants that have passed their prime in order to make room for new growth.

Effective Growing Season Again

For example, my first season I foolishly kept some tomatoes from the summer crop alive until past Thanksgiving — despite the fact that their maximum fruit production, which reached its peak in August, had long since passed. For the sake of a few pale and sickly tomatoes, I sacrificed valuable growing space which would have been better utilized for an autumn crop of peas, lettuce, spinach and cabbage. A few entries from that long ago greenhouse journal give the picture:

October 23 — Pulled squash plant from number two tank; it was about done and had aphids crawling all over it.

October 30 — Cold, windy and damp weather for the last two days. I am now feeding the plants only twice a day: AM and PM. Plants are not doing much these days — it's probably about over for them as far as much growth is concerned. Research the idea of waning photoperiod in addition to cold temperature as a factor in plant decline.

November 6 — All growth has slowed down to a standstill. Tomatoes take weeks to ripen, and then never get much beyond a pale salmon color. The cucumbers grow very, very slowly. Even the so-called cool weather crops are not growing — lettuce, spinach and Chinese Cabbage seedlings are still seedlings after almost a month.

November 21 — I pulled the tomato plant in tank number two — its leaves were mottled and beginning to turn yellow, and the main stem had weird warts all over it; there were only a few ugly and misshapen green fruits with splitting skins; the general vibes of the plant were very sick. One new sprout from the main stem near the roots looked healthy, so I left it to form a new plant.

November 22 — Removed the tomato at the rear of tank number seven — no more fruit. It was small and puny — never was much of a plant.

November 23 — Terminated the tomato in tank number three — similar reasons as above. Transplanted one head lettuce from number seven to number two, and endive from number three to number two. The root systems on both plants have not yet broken through the peat pot. These were planted as seedlings on October 18th — not much growth.

November 27 — The greenhouse thermometer shows thirty-two degrees F. this AM — the plants aren't frozen, but they don't look very happy. The tomato in number seven is getting yellow leaves.

November 28 — Thanksgiving day. It got down to thirty-two degrees F. again last night. The cucumber looks as if some of its leaves froze. Lettuce plants (planted October 18) are now three to five inches high; still just seedlings. Spinach plants (same date) are only two-and-a-half inches tall. Tomatos look as if they are dying of old age. All of the algae in the fish tank is dead and gone — too cold.

November 30 — Freeze out; it reached twenty-seven degrees F. last night. Everything seems done-in, though the lettuce and spinach might pull through. This afternoon I pulled all plants except the seedlings in two, four and five.

January 4 — Pulled the last of the lettuce — it was frozen solid.

These notes confirm the information found in Figure 2-1 on page 16, as well as suggest some improved management techniques. Let's take each pertinent entry and, with the gift of hindsight, analyze what I did wrong.

Cool and Warm Season Crops

To begin with, the October 23rd entry was made two days past the end of the effective growing season as shown in Figure 2-1 on page 16. The fact that I pulled a warm season plant like squash so late in the cycle, indicates that I'd not yet learned to manage the greenhouse efficiently. Any plant should be terminated just as soon as it passes its peak in productivity — for warm season crops like tomatos, squash and cucumbers, this would be sometime in August in my section of the country. As soon as the tanks are free, cool season crops like lettuce, spinach, peas and cabbage should be planted. This gives the new seedlings a chance to get off to a good start before the coming colder weather and shorter days have a chance to slow them down. Seedlings which do not put on rapid growth during their first few weeks seldom amount to much as plants. Don't waste your time trying to nurse recalcitrant seedlings into health — it's usually best to pull them and start over with fresh stock. Your increasing experience with the system will eventually tell you when this is advisable.

The fact that the squash plant referred to in the October 23rd entry was infested with aphids also suggests that it was past its prime. I have found that insects do not tend to infest healthy young plants. If a plant is infested with insects, it is usually either old, unhealthy to begin with, or most likely, both. I am not speaking here of a few aphids crawling on a few leaves, but of actual infestations of many hundreds of insects.

Feeding Schedule

In the entry for October 30th, it is noted that the plants are now only fed twice a day. Actually, the three-times a day schedule could have been terminated a month earlier. Multiple feedings are necessary only during the hot days of summer to prevent wilting, but in cooler periods of the year there is little need for it. In spring and autumn I fed the plants in the morning when I got up, and again around three o'clock in the afternoon. This varies according to weather conditions; on unusually hot days, three feedings may be in order, whereas on cold, cloudy days one may be all that is required. Many references on hydroponic gardening state that only one feeding per day is required. Since my experience has been otherwise, particularly in the summer, I can only suggest that each grower do what seems best for his or her specific conditions. Suffice it to say that when the plants begin to droop and wilt, feeding is in order.

The entry for November 6th confirms what was said earlier — warm weather plants such as tomatoes and cucumbers require minimum temperatures of sixty degrees F. for optimum growth. A glance at Figure 5-1 on page 43 tells us that the greenhouse low average temperature for the month of Scorpio (Oct. 21 to Nov. 21) was only 41 degrees — nineteen degrees colder than the minimum. The fact that the lettuce, spinach and Chinese Cabbage seedlings mentioned here are not growing well can be attributed to the fact that they were planted only three days before the October 21st cut-off date.

The remaining entries give the details of what one can expect during the winter "growing season" with an unheated greenhouse and no photoperiod supplement. If you are content with an eight-month greenhouse, then October 21st is the end of your gardening, and you must wait until the 21st of February before any practical plant growth can again be expected. I have outlined how adequate temperature control and artificial lighting can overcome these handicaps, but the added trouble and expense for such measures must be weighed against their advantages.

Experience is the Best Teacher

There is just no substitute for experience in hydroponic greenhouse gardening, and since I have found that my experience sometimes contradicts the information found in the literature on the subject, you may find that some of my techniques won't work under your specific conditions. I've learned not to worry about this phenomenon — the world is full of experts who contradict each other, and while it is valuable to read everything you can get about a subject, the expert's information is only as useful as its applicability to your own experience. Never be afraid to experiment, and don't worry too much if your definition of reality doesn't jibe exactly with someone else's — it's a phenomenon basic to the human condition.

I will now discuss my experience with the pit greenhouse as an eight-month growing structure. The following planting schedules should be considered as points of departure only; unless your environmental conditions are quite similar to mine, I would expect that adjustments to your local eco-system will be necessary.

The Spring Crop

In my experience, February 21st is an almost magical day; for many years now it has been the date when plant growth again becomes noticeable after four months of dormancy. The seeds of cool weather crops may now be planted in the gravel tanks, or, if you wish to get an even bigger jump on the season, they may be started earlier in the house in peat pots for transplanting into the tanks as seedlings around the 21st.

Since the weather is still quite cold, your greenhouse will have to be heated, or at least well insulated. Several methods of accomplishing this have already been covered. One idea that might be worth trying is to use dark colored, even black, gravel as your root-support medium in the hydroponic tanks. Aggregate of any kind makes an excellent solar heat storage "battery," and since dark pigments absorb heat much more efficiently than light pigments, a black gravel would provide the seedlings with extra warmth around the roots. (Actually, ordinary light grey pea gravel will hold temperatures well above the freezing point, even with night time air temperatures dropping into the low twenties.)

Black gravel might be entirely too hot for the summer growing season, however, and nobody wants to be changing the gravel in their tanks twice a year. One way to avoid this would be to spray the leveled gravel surface of each tank with black paint before the spring seeds or seedlings were planted. Then, later in the cycle when temperatures get too hot, it could easily be raked over to change the dark surface back to a light one.

Cool Season Vegetables

The cool weather vegetables planted in spring and autumn are:
1. Lettuce (loose leaf) — 40 days
2. Spinach — 42 days
3. Swiss Chard — 60 days
4. Radish — 22 days
5. Chinese Cabbage — 70 days
6. Peas — 55 days
7. Turnips (for greens or roots) — 45 days

Always place the tallest growing plants (such as peas) at the rear of your tanks or in the hindmost trough, since then they cannot block the sunlight from the shorter vegetables. Until the peas grow tall enough to hide them, reflectors should be placed in such a way as to increase the light intensity. A good module is a sixteen-inch square of one-quarter inch plywood painted with flat white paint or covered with white mylar plastic. Your reflectors should be propped and angled enough to reflect the maximum amount of light on the plants. A small piece of white plastic "mulch" placed under each seedling will also help to reflect more light intensity to your early spring crop.

Radishes, one of the fastest growing vegetables, are inter-cropped among all of the other varieties in each tank. As soon as they mature, they are harvested, and other seeds are sown. I am continually looking for space to plant radishes, and for this reason keep a packet of seeds within reach at all times.

Transition to Warm Season Crop

Spinach, lettuce, Swiss Chard and Chinese Cabbage can all be trimmed as their outer leaves become large enough to eat, thus allowing more than one meal from the same plants. As the season progresses, however, you will want to begin making room for your warm season crops. If all of the above vegetables were planted around the 21st of February, you should begin eating spinach, lettuce and turnip greens about the first of April, with Swiss Chard and peas coming two weeks later.

The first of May is not too soon to begin planting tomato seedlings. (I don't recommend planting the tiny tomato seeds directly in the tank — it's too easy for them to get flushed around in the gravel and sprout where you don't want them to grow.) Your peas will probably still be producing at this time, however, so you'll have to decide if you want to pull them to make room for the tomatos. (Since tomatos are tall plants, they ought to always be placed, like the peas, where they won't shade the shorter species.) If your peas are still producing a lot, the tomatos can wait for a couple of weeks, though they should definitely be in by the 15th of May.

At the risk of being tedious, I must repeat that these data reflect my own particular conditions. Generally speaking, when the inside average low temperatures get near fifty degrees, the time to plant warm season crops has arrived.

Warm Season Vegetables

My favorite warm season crops are:

1. Tomatos — 70 days
2. Bell Peppers — 70 days
3. Snap Beans — 50 days
4. Cucumber — 70 days
5. Summer Squash — 60 days (All things being equal, growing squash in a greenhouse makes sense only when it isn't possible to grow them outside; they are very large and bushy plants, and probably take up more room than they're worth.)

These warm season crops are planted in addition to sufficient lettuce to provide summer salads, and, of course, enough radishes to fill up any odd spaces not already occupied. Readers familiar with the French Intensive method of gardening may recognize this rationale for planting the hydroponic beds, which is essentially: make every square inch of growing space productive. *The Postage Stamp Garden Book* (1975), by Duane Newcomb, is an excellent reference for this method of intensive planting.

Pollination

Most warm season vegetables are raised for fruits rather than foliage. This means that their flowers must be pollinated, and since the greenhouse is a more or less closed environment, the wind and insects which usually perform this vital function cannot be relied upon. Hand pollination is in order — a simple task which can be carried out during one's daily tour of the greenhouse.

Squash

For squash plants, with their large flowers, a feather makes a perfect pollinator. Pollen from the male flowers is gathered on the tip of the feather and transferred to the female flowers. The way to tell the difference between the two sexes is that the female blossom sprouts from the end of a tiny squash, whereas the male looks like an ordinary flower. The same holds for cucumber blossoms — the first time you see the difference, you'll never mistake them. Sometimes male flowers will be open when there are no females ready, and vice-versa. For this reason, it is helpful to have more than one squash plant, since the chances of both male and female flowers being open simultaneously are thereby increased. The drawback to this, of course, is that squash plants are very large, and take up an inordinate amount of greenhouse space. I usually pull my squash plants when those in the outside garden begin producing, thus making room in the tanks for less bulky vegetables.

Tomatoes

Tomatoes produce many more and much smaller flowers than squash, so the feather technique isn't as useful. The usual method of pollination is to just flick each flower lightly with your finger. If you hold a piece of black paper behind the flower as you do this, you'll be able to see the pollen as it is released.

One theory of effective greenhouse tomato production states that each plant's growing tip should be pinched off just as soon as the fifth truss has formed. The so-called "truss" is the little branch which holds the flowers, and ultimately, of course, the tomatoes themselves. Five trusses of tomatoes are about all one plant can efficiently produce within the space of the warm season growing period, and any further fruit set only takes energy away from them. Experienced tomato growers already know that the "suckers" which appear just between the main stem and the side branches should be removed as soon as they appear. If not, the plant becomes bushy with too much of its energy going into the production of useless foliage. Wittwer and Honma suggest that the circulation of air and carbon dioxide can be improved by regularly pruning the tomato leaves up to the level of the ripening fruit. This practice makes good sense, and certainly results in a neater looking greenhouse. It also leaves fewer hiding places for white flies and other insect pests to get started.

Cucumbers

Cucumbers usually produce many, many more male than female blossoms, and while they can be pollinated by hand, I have found that they always manage to pollinate themselves without any help. Perhaps the occasional breezes coming in the open vents are enough to do the trick. Unless you have an inordinate appetite for cucumbers, you're likely to find that one vine is more than enough to provide all you can eat in salads, plus a good surplus for making pickles. Cukes thrive especially well in hydroponic culture — sometimes they grow so fast that I have actually seen them move! A single vine can dominate a tremendous amount of space in a small greenhouse, and I never cease to marvel at the yearly cucumber jungle created by only one plant.

Reasonably stout string, stretched from the greenhouse rafters, is necessary to provide an adequate climbing support for your bean plants and cucumber vines. Try to run the string in such a way that the lush growth of these heavy producers won't shade the other crops too much. Some shading in a summer greenhouse can help to keep the temperatures from getting too hot, but too much shade will cut the growth of other plants. Once when I pulled a large squash plant in mid-summer, I planted a morning glory vine in the vacated space to provide a little color; it never grew enough to produce even one flower because the cucumber jungle in that part of the greenhouse blocked almost all of the sunlight. One strategy is to direct the vines outside via a ventilator opening, so that they won't shade such a large growing area. The same tactic could be used for melons, since at my altitude they are nearly impossible to raise in the outside garden, and are much too large a plant to grow in the greenhouse.

Transition to Fall Crop

By the 21st of August, most of the warm season crops will have passed their peak of productivity. This is the time to harden your heart and start pulling every plant that is past its prime in order to make room for the fall crop of cool weather vegetables. These will ordinarily be the same as your spring crop.

Maintenance of Hydroponic Chemicals

A hydroponic greenhouse, of course, requires some different maintenance routines than a conventional forcing structure. Since the technique uses the same solution over and over again, it is well adapted to arid climates. In Africa's Kalahari Desert, for example, an *outdoor* hydroponic facility uses only one-twentieth the amount of water required by conventional agriculture. Even so, the hydroponic solutions must be changed periodically, although I've found that this need not be done quite as often as some of the literature recommends. The commercial

chemical mixture that I started out with was *Hyponex* —
available in powder form from most nurseries. The manufacturer recommends changing chemicals weekly, although I've
found that they can be used with no apparent ill effect on the
plants for two weeks and longer. Even if you intend to use an
organic hydroponic solution, I recommend that you start with
a commercial chemical mixture to familiarize yourself with the
technique. Once you understand how it all works, you can begin
trying organic experiments. The plants grown in a correctly
prepared commercial solution will give you a standard of
comparison for the organic mix, so that when your organic
plants equal or outgrow the chemical ones, you'll know you are
doing it right.

Hydroponic Test Kit

If you are scientifically oriented, you might want to purchase
a hydroponic solutions testing kit. This is a specialized chemistry
set designed for use by commercial hydroponic greenhouses. It
will tell you the exact chemical breakdown in parts per million
of any nutrient solution — a useful thing to know when
formulating organic mixtures.

I purchased the La Motte Plant Nutrition Kit, Model AM-41
(Code 5406) from the La Motte Chemical Products Company,
Chestertown, MD 21620. However, not being the chemistry-set
type, I haven't used the kit as much as I could have, instead
relying on *The Complete Book of Composting* (Rodale), for its
average chemical analyses of various organic materials.

In rewriting this chapter, I again reviewed the literature about
hydroponics. Some of it, slanted toward the large commercial
growers, almost requires a degree in chemistry to understand. I
have not found the hydroponic method to be at all complicated
or difficult, though in writing a book about it I am aware that
conditions in other greenhouses might be different enough from

my own to cause problems. For example, I now use well water as the base of my solutions, and have never yet had any difficulties with pH or unwanted chemical content; in some areas, well water might be too "hard" (i.e., contain too high a concentration of dissolved mineral salts) to be useful as a base for a properly balanced hydroponic solution.

Most of the references recommend that growers have their water analyzed. Since the micronutrients often exist as impurities in the local water supply, it is a good idea to know where you are before you begin. Also, just because I've had no problems with pH doesn't mean that you won't. Since all of the references stress the importance of regular pH tests, I can only assume that perhaps I am fortunate in seldom having to make these adjustments in my hydroponic solutions. Not that it is all that difficult when I do.

Users of city water supplies might find it necessary to allow their water to set in an open vessel for a few days to allow the chlorine to dissipate. Also, the gravel beds should be flushed periodically with plain water to remove any build-up of impurities; I do this just before planting each new crop.

In the summer, when the plants are transpiring a lot, be prepared to top off each solution container with water every day. It is amazing how much water a plant can use up in a twenty-four hour period — the fast-growing cucumbers often use up more than a gallon a day in mid-summer.

In concluding this chapter, I can only say again that I am totally sold on hydroponics. Despite the chemical mumbo jumbo found in some of the literature, I have never raised so many vegetables so quickly with so little trouble.

10

Insect Control

The more you can do to prevent pests from getting started, the further ahead you will be. The first step in control is to be a good observer and identify the pests properly. Get a good 10X magnifying glass and carry it with you when you go into the greenhouse. Inspect the plants each day. You should take a close look at both tops and bottoms of leaves, the stems, and roots at least once a week. Many times you can eliminate pests if you find and manually kill the first few invaders before they get a foothold.

— John White, "Growing Basics,"
The Solar Greenhouse Book

Insects can become a serious threat to the health of green-house plants, and there is seldom an easy solution to the problem. I suppose I am fortunate in that the only common indoor pests I've had any real trouble with have been aphids and white flies. There are plenty of others. For example, spider mites, mealybugs and scale insects are particularly common green-house nuisances, although I've personally seldom encountered these in any great numbers. Aphids and white flies (the latter sometimes wryly referred to as "flying dandruff") are quite bad enough, however, and they can be very troublesome to eradicate once they get started.

"Ladybug, ladybug, fly away home..."

Once when aphids were getting the upper hand and my infected plants still had a few weeks of productivity left, I caught a dozen or so lady beetles (the common "ladybug") in a mason jar and turned them loose on some badly infested Bell Peppers; it was amazing to watch how quickly the little red and black predators began hunting for food. The irony is that most of us have such a sweet image of the "ladybug" — the friendly little critter that just about everyone sentimentalizes. If they grew as large as Volkswagens, however, we'd all be in big trouble, be-cause they are truly ferocious animals — little Godzillas of the garden.

Through a magnifying glass I watched a small herd of aphids quietly browsing on a pepper leaf — enlarged they looked like so many fat Wildebeests grazing on Africa's Serengetti plain. Then, over the leaf's horizon charged a sleek and shiny lady beetle, who immediately snatched the largest aphid in her jaws and began devouring it alive. The only difference between this and a scene from the African veldt was one of scale. The aphid struggled for perhaps a full minute, its legs wildly scrambling in the air; not until it was at least half eaten did the obviously painful contortions finally cease.

This is a scene that takes place many million times a day in our fields and gardens, and it is therefore an excellent stratagem to employ in the greenhouse. The biological control of insect pests by utilizing their natural predators and parasites is a proven method of greenhouse management which compares as well or better with the use of chemical pesticides under most circumstances.

You don't even have to catch them yourself — predator insects, such as lady beetles and Lacewings are available by mail order from many sources. (See the ads in the back of publications like *Organic Gardening and Farming Magazine* to find out where to get these creatures.)

One season I purchased about a pint of lady beetles and released them all in my pit greenhouse to combat a bad aphid infestation. (This is not something to do in an attached greenhouse, since you'd literally have them crawling in your ears and all over the house.) For several days it was difficult to work in there without stepping on them, because they swarmed everywhere. Within a week, however, they had destroyed virtually every aphid and, since there was then nothing left for them to eat, they exited via the open ventilators.

This points out one of the problems encountered with the use of predatory insects — when they reach their adult stage, they are usually difficult to keep around because they are then sexually mature and innately restless to use their new wings to "fly away home" — wherever that may be. It is in their larval or juvenile stages that many species of lady beetles (there are over three hundred different varieties of this insect) actually consume most of their victims. Suffice it to say that if you can manage to always keep some youngsters established in the greenhouse you will be assured of more or less continuous predation.

The difference between caterpillars and butterflies reminds us that the larval stages of most insects do not resemble the adults at all. This includes the lady beetle, the immature version of which resembles an ugly little orange and black alligator. I ruefully admit that before I knew what they were I used to kill them on sight, since they look exactly like something that would devour your plants. In my ignorance I was actually destroying one of the best allies one can have in the war against greenhouse pests.

Lest you think that this biological control of bad bugs might be overstated or idealistically impractical, I offer the following data as to the insatiable hunger of lady beetles:

> As large-type predators with voracious appetites, most lady beetles must consume a number of prey before they can get down to egg production. The nearly grown larva of *Stethorus punctum*, a predator of spider mites, will consume 100 to 400 mites per day. The convergent lady beetle consumes about 400 medium-size aphids during its larval growth; once it reaches adulthood, it requires another 300 aphids before it starts producing eggs, and then it needs 3 to 10 aphids for each egg laid. *One beetle may devour more than 5,000 aphids in its adult career.* So, lady beetles don't reproduce around skimpy prey populations. Big appetites reflect big needs. (Emphasis mine.)[1]

Lacewings

Another predator useful in bug control is the lacewing fly. These are sold commercially and, like lady beetles, are also commonly found outside in the wild during the summer. There are green and brown varieties, the green lacewing being the one usually sold by mail. The larval stage is carnivorous, and resembles the lady beetle larva (a "little alligator"), except that it is usually gray or gray green in coloration.

Adult green lacewings, in fact, have given up their predatory ways entirely, and subsist entirely on pollen and flower nectar. However, you'll still want to keep some adults around if you can, to ensure that they lay the eggs which will hatch out into ravenous "meat-eating" larvae. The green lacewing adult is easily identified — you've probably seen hundreds of them. It is a pale green insect, about three-quarters of an inch long, with long antennae, large transparent wings and prominent gold-colored eyes. They actually look rather innocuous and wimpy, sort of like mayflies — not at all like the vicious predators they are as juveniles. If you spot lacewings around your yard or garden it is well worth the trouble to capture as many as possible in a jar or can and release them in the greenhouse; like their lady beetle cousins, they are universally respected pest controllers:

> (Lacewings are) voracious predators that eat almost anything they can conquer: aphids, mealybugs, immature scales and whiteflies, the eggs of insects and mites, thrips and mites all make up the menu. One larva can consume more than 400 aphids during its growth. Unfortunately, other lacewing larvae can go on the menu, too, which creates problems for the control program. If they're not scattered well apart when set out as eggs, they eliminate many of themselves right after hatching and before attacking the pest species.[2]

White Fly Control

White flies are perennial greenhouse pests that you will probably be battling continuously. These innocent looking little bugs are actually very, very tiny moths, which in vast numbers can easily kill entire plants. I've never seen them outdoors, and god only knows where they come from: they seem to exist for the sole purpose of infesting greenhouses. Unfortunately, lady beetles don't seem to eat them.

I have often ruthlessly uprooted all plants infested with white fly; because these were almost invariably old cucumber plants, the losses weren't as great as might be supposed, since in most cases I'd already harvested the bulk of the crop. White flies *love* cucumbers, so one should constantly monitor these plants for any infestation.

The adults tend to stay around the tops of the plants where they lay their eggs. Strange as it may seem, the larvae are scale insects, and not easily recognized as "bugs" — in fact, they're practically microscopic. I always keep a powerful magnifying glass in the greenhouse and use it regularly to look for signs of white fly scale activity on plant leaves. Once the larvae become established, the leaves begin to grow pale and yellow, and finally fall off.

If white fly is detected early enough — before there are too many of them — spraying plain water on the leaves is sometimes effective. (Spraying your plants with water occasionally is a good practice anyway, and is a particularly effective remedy against spider mites.) Another technique that works pretty well is to suck up the adult white flies with a vacuum cleaner in one hand while you shake the plants with the other to make them fly. A small "Dust Buster" type hand vacuum is ideal for this task.

The parasitic wasp, *Encarsia formosa*, is an incredibly tiny creature — even smaller than its host, which is gnat-sized at best — but it has proven to be extremely effective in controlling white flies. Although I have not personally used these insects, commercial greenhouses all over the world employ *Encarsia formosa* as a standard white fly control strategy.

This exhausts my personal experience with ecological methods of bug management. Those readers who are interested in the field will find the book, *Windowsill Ecology*, by William H. Jordan, Jr. (Rodale, 1977), an invaluable source of information on these fascinating techniques of pest disposal.

Greenhouse Pesticides

Although biological control is certainly safer, more interesting and aesthetic than the application of pesticides, this isn't always a practical solution for every insect problem. It is at this point that the mettle of any organic gardener is really tested. It's one thing to give lip service to anti-pesticide sentiments, it's quite another to see your greenhouse being taken over by millions of white flies. I confess that I have occasionally compromised my higher principles and sprayed infested plants with poisons; so has just about every other greenhouse gardener I know. Almost invariably, white fly was the problem.

In my experience, *Rotenone*, a so-called "safe" pesticide, was totally ineffective, as was *Malathion*, a not-so-safe insect killer. However, I have had good success with *PT 1200 Resmethrin*, a commercial greenhouse aerosol which is custom made for white fly control; this pesticide, a synthetic pyrethrum formula, is not generally available for anything but "professional use," although so far I've experienced no trouble as a "private citizen" in purchasing it from greenhouse supply dealers. (It says on the can: "For sale to, use, and storage by servicepersons," whatever that means.).

One major drawback is that you *absolutely cannot* use it while there are fish or rabbits in the greenhouse, and according to the instructions on the can, you must use a respirator while applying it. ("Keep greenhouse closed 2-4 hours, preferably over night following treatment. All human occupants and pets must be removed from the greenhouse before treatment is started. Occupants should not re-enter the building until it has been ventilated.") Fish are particularly vulnerable to pyrethrum-based pesticides: even minute quantities in the low parts-per-million range can be fatal. Obviously, I did not use any kind of chemical insect control while I was conducting my aquaculture experiments.

For all that, I've never gotten the feeling that *Resmethrin* is significantly more dangerous to humans than other sprays you can buy in an aerosol can, although there must be a good reason why it isn't readily available to the general public. Most pesticides really are dangerous, so you should take that into account before using this or any bug killer. Whatever your feelings about this subject are, the fact remains that *Resmethrin* is absolutely lethal to adult white flies.

Sources

1. *Windowsill Ecology*, Jordan, William H., Jr., Rodale Press, Emmaus, PA, 1977. p. 94.

2. *Ibid.*, p. 87

11

Aquaculture

I'm not convinced that fish culture is for everybody, not even for everybody with solar greenhouses.
— William McLarney, Personal communication 2/9/91

Aquaculture is the intensive cultivation of fish or other cold-blooded aquatic animals, such as mussels, clams and crayfish, under optimum growing conditions. Fish farming has been practiced for thousands of years in the Orient, and has recently become a profitable business in the United States. Catfish are raised on large farms in the Ozarks and southern states, and in Louisiana and Texas alone over thirty-five thousand tons of crayfish are produced each year. In the mountain states such as Idaho, where an abundance of cold running water is available, fish farms provide the market with pan-sized Rainbow trout at premium prices.

In this country, aquaculture, like most other farming, is usually run along agribusiness lines, with an eye toward maximum yields and profits. In many instances, fish are "packed like sardines" in ponds or cages in which the water is constantly circulated, filtered and aerated to keep the inhabitants from immediately expiring in their own waste products. These fish feedlots make use of high-protein "chows" manufactured by the major livestock ration companies, and hence bear no relationship at all to the organic low-energy aquaculture operations of the Orient — which, interestingly enough, are said to consistently out-produce the high-tech methods normally used in America.

Advantages of Aquaculture

The rationale behind fish farming is a very compelling one indeed:

> The best argument for aquaculture is based on the ever-increasing need for protein foods. Fishes and aquatic invertebrates are far more efficient food converters than their warm-blooded counterparts, since they need expend little or no energy supporting their weight or maintaining their body temperatures. *They are thus capable of producing more protein per unit area from the same amount of food.*[1] (Emphasis mine.)

This makes a lot of sense, which becomes particularly emphasized when we examine the warm-blooded side of the equation:

> Warm-blooded land animals are monstrously inefficient producers of nutritious food, and their meat will become more and more of a luxury as the population increases and

good agricultural land becomes more scarce. *Almost 90 percent of the food given to beef cattle, for example, is "wasted" because it is used to keep up the animal's body temperature.* The harvest of protein food in the form of meat is small in return for the corn, grain and hay that is invested in supporting the animals.[2] (Emphasis mine.)

The weight-gaining efficiency of cold-blooded aquatic animals, plus the heat-retaining properties of water make aquaculture a very attractive component of an eco-system greenhouse, since the water mass used to buffer winter temperatures can also be utilized for another protein crop. Every inch of precious greenhouse space is thereby used to maximum advantage. It is a truly elegant idea.

The fact that it is a great idea doesn't mean that it is necessarily easy or practical to do. Much of the early enthusiasm for solar greenhouse aquaculture, most of it generated by the New Alchemy Institute back in the '70s, has bogged down in the realities of providing for the unique needs of fish in artificial environments.

Fish, like plants, and all living organisms, must be provided with a subtle range of specific requirements if they are to attain optimum growth, and these prerequisites, like everything else in an eco-system, quickly branch out into an intricate tangle of inter-relationships. Because they are adapted to an aquatic world which is alien to us, fish require many life essentials which are not immediately obvious.

Requirements of Aquatic Life

The first thing any organism needs is space to live. In nature a given body of water will support an optimum number of fish; such an environment would be said to be in balance when the food, oxygen supply and water temperature are all at an adequate level to support this theoretically ideal population. All four factors (space, temperature, food and oxygen) are interrelated with the fifth factor of population density.

The most obvious difference between an intensive aquaculture operation and a natural environment is that nature never allows the population densities possible in a managed system. To this extent, our eco-system really isn't an "eco-system" at all, since we are eliminating all possible factors which would prohibit maximum production of selected plant and animal species. We are the only predators in our eco-system, and we see to it that every condition is met for the highest yields attainable. While each carp living in a natural body of water might have thousands of gallons of water at its disposal, that same fish in an intensive aquaculture system might have only one gallon or less!

Aquaculture at
the Max Planck Institute

At the Max Planck Institute in Germany, for example, scientists have succeeded in raising *ten* two-pound carp in *one* ten-gallon aquarium! The fish are so crowded that their backs are out of the water, and they are effectively unable to move more than an inch or two in any direction. In order to accomplish such a feat, vast amounts of energy must be pumped into the system; the temperature-controlled water is continuously circulated, aerated, and filtered, and the fish fed a certain percentage of their weight each day with a ration of specially formulated food. When one considers the real cost of such an operation, it becomes obvious that these fish dinners are a "heat sink" — that is, they require more energy to produce than they give back in food.

The Real Costs

It is for this reason that I am extremely skeptical when I read about schemes for raising trout in urban basements. The environmental cost of the electricity required to continuously pump, filter and control the temperature of the water, not to mention the fact that commercial fish chows are largely composed of other fish caught in foreign waters, make such schemes as environmentally unsound as the worst agribusiness practices.

Aeration and Filtration

Fish in close confinement, as anyone who has ever raised tropical fish knows, require constantly aerated and filtered water to survive. Just as a large number of people confined in a small, tightly closed room would quickly become sick in the stale air unless adequate ventilation were provided, so a lot of fish in a small tank will suffer from lack of oxygen in their water. (For some perspective: the infamous "Black Hole of Calcutta" refers to an incident in 1756 in which 146 people were confined overnight in a room 18 by 14 feet with only two small windows for ventilation. In the morning only 23 were still alive.)

In addition to this, fish crowded in a small space will excrete growth-inhibiting chemicals called metabolites which prevent normal growth no matter how much the fish are fed. For this reason, the fish tank water must be constantly filtered to remove these toxins.

To accomplish these functions in a closed system, the water has to be circulated rapidly enough to filter out the metabolites as fast as they are produced, and replace the oxygen as fast as it is consumed. This implies the use of large amounts of electricity to run the circulation pump, and as I have mentioned before, the use of solar or wind-electric systems generally precludes such a continuous high wattage drain on the battery storage system.

Temperature

Like plants, fish also require certain optimum levels of temperature if they are to grow enough to pay for their keep. U.S. Department of Agriculture Bulletin No. 2244, *Catfish Farming*, states:

> Catfish grow rapidly if properly fed and if the water temperature is 70 degrees F. or more. Growth is slow between 60 and 70 degrees F. Little growth occurs when water is colder than 60 degrees.[3]

Trout, on the other hand, are cold water fish which don't thrive in temperatures much *higher* than 60 degrees F. Since the rationale of aquaculture in an eco-system greenhouse is to cleverly utilize the passive liquid heating system for yet another protein crop, warm water fish are obviously the type we want to raise; it defeats our purpose to attempt to raise cold water fish in a hot-house.

Food — Carnivorous fish

Fish must be fed, and since (as long as we are playing the eco-system game), the ecologically unsound commercial chows are out of the question, that means we must produce our own fish food. Carnivorous fish, such as bluegill, catfish, perch and crappie, require a high protein diet of insects, earthworms, aquatic invertebrates, etc., which can all be cultivated with varying degrees of difficulty.

My first (and as it has turned out to date, only) experiments were with carnivores. Since the bluegill sunfish was the only locally available species I knew about at the time, these were what I went for. In May of 1974 I filed the barbs off several fish hooks, half filled two 55-gallon drums with water, and set off for the nearest pond. In about two hours I managed to catch fifty-five small bluegills. (I was going on the hypothesis that one fish per gallon of unaerated holding container was a safe temporary population density.) I quickly transported these captives back home and released them in the 1,400 gallon greenhouse tank; they all survived the trip without any casualties.

Earthworms

Recent studies have indicated that earthworms are actually nutritionally superior to commercial trout and catfish rations, so I was on good ground in using them to feed the bluegills. Further encouragement came from an article in the November, 1973 issue of *Organic Gardening* entitled, "Raising catfish in a barrel,"[4] which described an earthworm feeding system for catfish. Since I already had four 55-gallon drum-halves planted with earthworms and compost, I felt that I was well on my way to becoming a fish farmer.

Then, the "there's no such thing as a free lunch" law began to assert itself. In working with the eco-system greenhouse I've had this law enforced many times. The fact is inescapable: you can't get something for nothing.

What happened was that the fish were constantly hungry. The more I fed them, the more they ate, until my supply of earthworms couldn't keep up with the demand. When I re-read the "catfish in a barrel" article, I discovered that the authors were commercial earthworm raisers — an extremely significant fact that I hadn't previously considered.

Obviously, my four pitiful little compost bins were totally inadequate for producing the number of worms that were necessary for a productive aquaculture system. If one figures a minimum growth diet of five worms per fish per day, one winds up using (assuming 55 fish) 275 per day, 1,925 per week, 7,700 per month and 46,200 every six months. If you had to purchase this food, at a cost in this area of $20.00 per 7,000 earthworms, those fish dinners begin to be anything but a "free lunch" — they don't even qualify as a cheap lunch! Assuming an *optimistic* harvest weight of one-quarter pound of edible meat per fish, and a 90-day growing cycle, the fish would end up costing more than four dollars per pound. As of this writing, one can purchase trout and catfish in the supermarket at near half this price. In purely economic terms, one would be ahead by selling the worms and buying twice the number of fish with the proceeds! The solution, of course, is to create a much larger worm farm — one in which the creatures' natural reproduction is able to keep up with the need for fish food. The New Alchemists claim to get a minimum of 400 worms per day from a box eight feet square by three feet deep. They have also gotten good results by artificially raising midge and mosquito larvae in numbers large enough to provide a significant protein supplement for tilapia.

Bug Light

Meanwhile, in an effort to ease the demand on my hard-pressed earthworms, I attached a 12-volt tail-light bulb to the wind-electric system, hung it over the fish tank each night during the summer, left the door and all vent flaps open, and used the light to attract insects for the fish to eat. This system worked very well. Although I was apprehensive about bringing such visitors into the greenhouse, I needn't have worried. The bluegills must have eaten virtually every one of them, because I had no problems with insect damage to the plants. It became a kind of meditation to "watch the fish eat." Each evening one could see the bluegills grouped in a huge circle around the light, waiting for any bug foolish enough to come within striking distance. Each morning a thin film of "left-overs" — insect wings, legs, etc. — covered the water.

That solution worked well enough for the summer months, but when the nights began to cool off and the bug population dwindled, it was back to an earthworm diet for the fishes. When we finally harvested them in the autumn of 1974 they had put on virtually no growth at all.

By then, of course, I'd discovered that the wind-electric system couldn't possibly handle the load for water circulation, but with a density of only one fish for each 25 gallons of water, I wasn't overly worried about aeration and filtration.

Food — Herbivorous Fish

For obvious reasons, my thoughts next began to turn to non-carnivorous species. Herbivorous fish, like tilapia and amurs, will thrive on a diet of algae, aquatic plants, and even carrot tops — clearly an easier diet to produce than worms and bugs. Tilapia, the species advocated by the New Alchemy Institute, are native to Africa and the Near East. In addition to being plant eaters, they are extremely prolific. Another species mentioned in the aquaculture literature is the white amur, or grass carp, which is native to the Orient. Said to be voracious vegetarians, amurs can reportedly reach weights of up to 70 pounds in a relatively short period of time. In addition, they are not temperature sensitive, and can survive in very cold water. (Tilapia will die if water temperatures go much below 50 degrees F.) Amurs are also said to be a gourmet delicacy, prized for their flavor. On the down side, they won't breed in captivity, and are illegal to import into many states. (For sound reasons: the last thing that any local ecosystem needs is the "accidental" introduction of another exotic species into its waterways.)

This left tilapia as the only logical choice, but since these fish can't live in cold water and won't even grow in water less that 70 degrees F., it meant some modifications to my thinking. Obviously, they would have to be a seasonal, not a year-round crop.

A Fifty-Five Gallon Drum Aquarium

After reading about the intensive carp culture experiments at the Max Planck Institute in Germany, I decided to try a modified version of their technique. Instead of raising ten carp in a ten-gallon aquarium, why couldn't I raise twenty tilapia in a 55-gallon drum?

(It is, of course, not essential to use a 55-gallon drum — that was just the convenient proletarian module I favored at the time. The New Alchemists have pioneered the use of fiberglass cylinders of varying capacities, which could easily be outfitted with both the heating and circulation systems described below.)

I reasoned that 55 gallons was a small enough volume of water to be handled by both the wind-electric system and the small solar panel I originally employed. This was a "Solarator," a small wading-pool heater which is probably not even manufactured anymore. The manufacturer stated that it would heat up to ten-thousand gallons of water, but significantly, he didn't state to what temperature. Of course, 55 gallons of water wouldn't do much toward heating the greenhouse, but by then I was only interested in making some method of aquaculture work for me.

I decided to use the principle of the aquarium, familiar to tropical fish fanciers. A false bottom, consisting of a round piece of corrugated plastic roofing material, was placed in the 55-

gallon drum. This was equipped with four pieces of PVC pipe — two to admit a constant stream of compressed air, two to allow it to escape from the bottom of the tank. A four-inch layer of crushed oyster shell was placed on top of the corrugated false bottom, and holes drilled at one-inch intervals along the corrugations allowed for the circulation of water. When compressed air enters the system — in addition to providing oxygen for the fish — it causes a current to draw the water through the crushed oyster shell. Aerobic bacteria living in this material devour the growth-inhibiting metabolites produced by the fish. For those readers unfamiliar with this process, it is identical to the life-support system used in home aquariums.

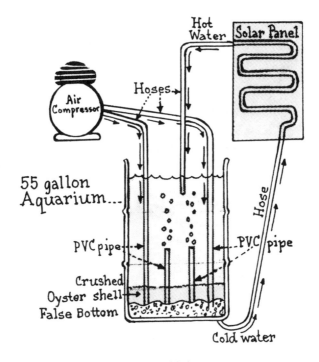

Figure 11-1

Schematic for greenhouse aquarium.

The compressed air was provided by a 12-volt air compressor used in recreational vehicles. A valve on the air tank metered out the small amount needed to keep the system going. Since the compressor shut itself off when the tank pressure reached 40 psi, it was not required to run all of the time. When the tank pressure dropped to 20 psi, the compressor automatically started up again. The idea was loosely inspired by the way an air tank set-up works in home water well systems. If we assume the 60-watt compressor runs only fifteen minutes every hour, we would only be drawing about 10.8 KWH a month. At least, that was my theory.

The plan called for the tank to be heated by a separate system. A thermostat placed at the solar panel would automatically turn on a tiny 12-volt Recreational Vehicle water pump which pumps two gallons per minute, and only draws 18-watts. Water is pumped from the bottom of the tank when the solar panel thermostat registers 120 degrees F. The pump is turned off when the solar panel temperature drops to 80 degrees F. Another thermostat at the top of the tank shuts the entire system down when the tank temperature reaches 85 degrees F. The system is activated again when the tank temperature drops to 70 degrees F.

Now I must hasten to say that I never got quite this far with the idea, since the RV air compressor burned out the first day I hooked it up to a regular ten-gallon aquarium. (This was a preliminary test to see how the system worked.) Alas, twelve-volt equipment, generally designed for occasional and intermittent use, is often not suitable for the kinds of loads the appropriate technology experimenter wants to put on it.

Let me summarize the frustrating conclusion of this tale. After considerable fooling around, exacerbated by other, non-aquaculture-related circumstances, I was finally forced to abandon the project in great disgust. The little 200-watt wind generator I was using at that time was just not capable of supplying the power I needed for even the minimum functioning of the system as originally designed.

In theory, the idea of home greenhouse aquaculture is an elegant one; in practice, I have not yet found it to be so easy to realize. Anyone who has ever raised tropical fish in an aquarium has probably experienced the wide range of problems that can plague fish culturists. The essence of the problem can be stated as follows:

> So poor has been the fish man's understanding of the complicated interactions between the fish and its watery element that he has failed to recognize *bad water as the underlying cause of most of his failures*... Aquatic animals change the chemistry of their culture water. Their physiology is in turn affected by these changes, usually in adverse ways... The major concept presented is that *accumulating toxic metabolites are the primary limiting factors in aquatic animal culture and that removing them on a continuous basis should be the foremost objective in routine water management*... The size of a culture system has little bearing on the isolation and solution of water management problems. These are essentially the same in a 10-gallon aquarium or a 10-million-gallon hatchery... *Captive animals are at the mercy of their limited environment.*[5] (Emphasis mine.)

We see here the subtle yet crucial difference between the commercially successful kind of aquaculture practiced outdoors in ponds, rivers, etc., and the largely problematic aquaculture common to artificial closed systems, such as aquariums and tanks in greenhouses. When working with intensive culture in small closed systems, large amounts of energy must be utilized to compensate for the inherent buffers that nature provides in large natural bodies of water. The cost of providing this energy simply may not be cost effective in a small system.

There was a great surge of interest in aquaculture back in the 1970s, much of it generated by the enthusiastic literature published by the New Alchemy Institute in Woods Hole, Massachusetts. I was (and still am) captivated by their concepts and their idealism, which holds forth the promise of a sane and sustainable agriculture based on ecological principles.

Unfortunately, in reviewing their literature for the new edition of this book, I began to see a pattern emerge that had eluded me in my original enthusiasm for the sheer elegance of their ideas. Much of the New Alchemy material is vague in the extreme — it ranks very high in creatively idealistic projections, yet very little hard data is presented. The following quotations are typical:

> The yields from the aquaculture have been excellent, while in winter, in the greenhouse, we have grown cash crops to maturity.[6]

First, what constitutes an "excellent" aquaculture yield? Second, what "cash crop" can they be speaking of? I know of no *commercial* greenhouse that raises cash crops to maturity in the wintertime, so if the Alchemists are doing it, I want to know all of the details. Unfortunately, few details are given in most of the New Alchemy literature I've seen to date:

> We feel cautiously optimistic about economic microfarms like the Ark. This is borne out of several breakthroughs we've had at New Alchemy that particularly involve the Cape Cod Ark. The first of these involves our success in the miniaturized terrestrial and aquatic ecosystems in the Ark that have been created without a loss in biological integrity. *This is perhaps best illustrated by the solar-algae ponds, which sustain fish populations as dense as 3 per gallon, and also by the intensive indoor gardens that produce crops throughout all seasons without recourse to machinery, chemical applications, or auxiliary fuels.* This was accomplished through ecological complexity, space-fitting plant-structural relationships, and the presence of

light-reflecting surfaces within the bioshelter.[7] (Emphasis mine)

Fish populations of "three per gallon" may sound impressive until you note that no mention is made of their size. Most home aquariums hold more than three fish per gallon — of course these are generally the size of guppies! The same point can be made of this quotation:

> The aquaculture in the solar-algae ponds is productive. Yields have been more than an order of magnitude higher than any others recorded for still-water aquaculture, going as high with tilapia as 15 kilograms/tank/year.[8]

This is a very impressive claim, yet it does not provide the data needed to evaluate it. For example, 15 kilograms of fish only one inch long would fit this description, yet be an essentially worthless crop from the standpoint of human consumption. We need to know how many fish of edible size are produced and what are the costs and requirements needed to produce them. I have yet to see this kind of hard data published by the Alchemists, and its absence is damaging to their credibility. Surely, if their accomplishment was as great as they claim it is, they could logically be expected to produce hard evidence along with instructions on how to reproduce it, and, most importantly, others would be emulating their techniques.

To the best of my knowledge, to date, intensive greenhouse aquaculture has not lived up to the lavish claims made for it back in the seventies. In an aquaculture bulletin dated 12/88, the New Alchemy Institute seems to finally acknowledge this:

> Costs associated with indoor freshwater aquaculture today are simply too high to justify a continued emphasis on this subject... Our emphasis has shifted to organic agriculture research and demonstration, education, and resource-efficient greenhouses and housing.

None of this means that it can't be done. Aquaculture is a very new concept in the United States — less than forty years old — so raising practical quantities of inexpensive aquatic protein in a small closed system remains a worthy challenge in and of itself. My current position is that one should first master the biological problems before adding to them the handicap of restricted energy sources. (It must be noted, however, that modern photovoltaic technology *in theory* should be capable of providing the power needs of a well-designed small aquaculture system.)

As of this writing, early 1991, nearly sixteen years after the original experiments, I have yet to resume the investigation. However, I recently purchased a fifty-gallon glass aquarium and will soon renew the undertaking under the set of assumptions noted above. That is, I intend to master the culture of the fish before trying to raise them with an alternative energy system. When one considers the price of fish at the supermarket, as well as the sad fact that many of them come from polluted waters, it may still prove to be cost effective to raise fish in a greenhouse using conventional power sources. This is a big movement from my original thinking on the subject, and only my love of seafood inspires such heresy.

Perhaps we only need to reorganize our thinking on the subject. Recently it occurred to me that one of the most common experiences of warm water fishermen is that of catching dozens of undersized pan-fish (bluegill, crappie, etc.) for every edible specimen. These "runts" are usually unceremoniously thrown ashore, dumped in the garbage, or otherwise wasted. If one were to carefully save these small fishes in a portable tank and transport them home to a large aquarium, it seems to me that they could be fattened up for the table in a fairly short time. (I understand that 12-volt aerators are available for holding tanks, so one could safely accumulate a fair number of fish during any given expedition.) Thus, it isn't necessary to think in terms of breeding fish for continuous production in an aquaculture system — one only needs to utilize what is now a largely wasted resource by using an aquarium or other tank as a kind of green-house "feed lot" for immature fishes. I intend to solve the feed problem by exploring the use of dry cat food, which is easily available, relatively inexpensive and high in protein. Although far from "ecological," this may prove more "economical" than feeding cats with it.

Update

As this book goes to press, I have just begun the experiment outlined above. My youngest son came home several days ago with a live ten-inch rock bass that he caught in a nearby reservoir. This species is not an ideal fish to raise in an aqua-culture system because it is a consummate predator, but we use what we have around here. The first thing I noted is that "Rocky" is insatiable — we watched in wonder as he consumed seventeen earthworms in a row! The second observation is that he will not *eat* cat food. Indeed, it seems that he will rather starve than do so. This puts a serious, perhaps fatal, limitation on my concept of practical greenhouse aquaculture — nobody I know has the time to be out digging worms in such numbers. Unless we can come up with a more practical food source, Rocky will probably be taken back to the reservoir — he's now a family pet, and none of us would think of eating him, which constitutes another limitation, of course. Most people would have to be close to starvation before they considered devouring their pets. It's much easier to be a carnivore when you aren't on a first-name basis with your food.

Sources

1. "Aquaculture on the organic farm and homestead," *Organic Gardening and Farming*, W. McLarney, August, 1971.

As this book goes to press, I have just begun the experiment outlined above. My youngest son came home several days ago with a live ten-inch rock bass that he caught in a nearby reservoir. This species is not an ideal fish to raise in an aquaculture system because it is a consummate predator, but we use what we have around here. The first thing I noted is that "Rocky" is insatiable — we watched in wonder as he consumed seventeen earthworms in a row! The second observation is that he will not *eat* cat food. Indeed, it seems that he will rather starve than do so. This puts a serious, perhaps fatal, limitation on my concept of practical greenhouse aquaculture — nobody I know has the time to be out digging worms in such numbers. Unless we can come up with a more practical food source, Rocky will probably be taken back to the reservoir — he's now a family pet, and none of us would think of eating him, which constitutes another limitation, of course. Most people would have to be close to starvation before they considered devouring their pets. It's much easier to be a carnivore when you aren't on a first-name basis with your food.

Sources

1. "Aquaculture on the organic farm and homestead," *Organic Gardening and Farming*, W. McLarney, August, 1971.
2. "Editorial," *Organic Gardening and Farming*, R. Rodale, April, 1971.
3. *Catfish Farming, a New Farm Crop*, R. Grizzel, Jr., et. al., USDA Farmer's Bulletin #2244, 1969.
4. "Raising catfish in a barrel," *Organic Gardening and Farming*, P. and J. Mahan, November, 1973.

12

Afterword
— Back to the Future

The end of the ocean came late in the summer of 1979, and it came even more rapidly than the biologists had expected. There had been signs for more than a decade, commencing with the discovery in 1968 that DDT slows down photosynthesis in marine plant life... Other changes had taken place in 1975. Most ocean fishes that returned to freshwater to breed, like the salmon, had become extinct, their breeding streams so damned [sic?] up and polluted that their powerful homing instinct only resulted in suicide...

— Paul Ehrlich, "Eco-Catastrophe!,"
Ramparts, September, 1969

If there is one fact that emerges from even the slightest study of history, let's say even from the turn of the century, it is that what happens comes as a surprise to everyone.

— Doris Lessing

Prophecy is too inexact to be a "science," yet it would be very difficult to plan our lives without some notion of what the future might hold in store for us. Consciously or unconsciously we make predictions every day and live our lives based on the expectations they engender. The future appears tantalizingly predictable because it is based upon our experience of the past, which, in retrospect, always seems quite comprehensible. Hindsight is 20/20, as the saying goes.

Yet the present is all that we can ever really know — even our memories of the past are experienced in the present and formed by continuously changing beliefs about what we think happened. That, plus what we think is happening now, becomes transformed somehow into what we think *will* happen: a belief, accurate or inaccurate, about the future. We have learned that cause and effect is a generally predictable equation for most life situations, hence we project into the future many plausible scenarios based upon it. Yet without an adequate knowledge of the infinity of hidden variables affecting the unfolding of time and events, these forecasts can be little more than educated guesses.

Experience seems to prove that the predictions of scientifically oriented observers (futurists) are hardly more accurate than the prophecies of seers and mystics. Based on results, futurists may legitimately be placed in the same category as astrologers: sometimes they're right, sometimes they're wrong, but no one will know for certain until the present moment finally catches up with the prediction.

Dr. Paul Ehrlich's doomsday scenarios from the sixties and seventies must have influenced the lives of many people — I know they influenced mine. Scary stuff about the ocean "dying" in 1979, written by a scientist presumably current with all of the latest information, is a powerful potion to swallow for those of us who tend to take life more seriously than perhaps we should.

It is now nearly sixteen years since the first edition of *The Survival Greenhouse* appeared in response to my absolute certitude that the world was going to fall apart within a matter of months — maybe a year or two at the most. I was hardly alone in my convictions — there were many of us in those days working toward a saner future, a future worth surviving for. To *want* to survive is a healthy statement of faith in the life-enhancing potential within the unfolding of time: Things *can* be better — we don't *have* to live this way.

However, during the recent interval that history labels "the Reagan years" our incipient environmental awareness dozed off into a curious sleep of self-indulgence in which most ecological issues were ignored. Indeed, we still have all of our original problems, plus a few more. The planet now hosts more than five billion human entities, a hole in the ozone layer has been discovered, the concept of global warming (the "greenhouse effect") is one of the latest things to worry about, the rain forests of the world are shrinking daily, and yet the human species is not only holding its own, it is proliferating like crazy!

So what happened to all those catastrophe scenarios from the sixties and seventies? Needless to say, the ocean didn't die in 1979, and needless to say the world didn't starve to death in 1983. Like the "Boy Who Cried Wolf" in the ancient fable, those who prophesied cataclysm appear ridiculous to the "business as usual" types who believe we're living in the best-of-all-possible-worlds right now. Were we gullible fools to have taken those doomsday forecasts seriously?

I don't think so. I think that the "catastrophe" has already happened, and that in some strange way it is even *worse* than those envisioned by the prophets. It is worse because to me the evidence implies that most human beings are not capable of rational choice or action. As a species we seem to be much less enlightened than our self-given title of *Homo Sapiens* would suggest. Although the doomsayers may have been off in their predictions by a decade or two, their reasons for dismay, trepidation and dread were (and still are!) legitimate ones.

No one can say that we weren't warned in time. There was at least some opportunity to turn the ecological juggernaut around during the seventies and eighties, yet collectively we did little or nothing. That suggests to me that the inevitable crunch, when it finally comes, will be much worse than predicted. Based on results, human beings apparently need to be pushed to the wall before they will act in their own best interests.

But even if the powers-that-be manage to hold it all together, even if we can somehow maintain our consumerist appetites indefinitely, the prospect of living on a planet clogged with the persons and detritus of five billion (and counting) human egos must be reckoned as an aesthetic catastrophe, if nothing else. Alas, we already have that with us right now — today. To rephrase Sartre: Hell is other people's taste and values.

I closed the first edition of this book with these thoughts:

> ...The root of all our problems are more moral and political than anything else. All of the alternative energy systems in the world will count for very little unless we can change the way in which we perceive ourselves and our environment. It isn't a matter of replacing one energy source with another, or exchanging types of hardware — the crux of the problem is how we perceive ourselves and our world. That is a question that each individual must answer for himself, and it is the aggregate of individual answers which will determine nothing less than how we shall live in the future.

That was written on September 29, 1975 — almost sixteen years ago. As I try to organize my thoughts to conclude this third edition, I am drawn to the *letters to the editor* column of the July-August, 1991 issue of *The Futurist* magazine. In a comment on a previous article written in the March-April issue by Jon Roland, Steve Wrubleski observes:

> ...No technological changes will compensate for a lack of human spiritual values. ...Until some threshold percentage of the population evolves a cultural structure oriented around a maturation of the heart and mind — until we evolve to a truly higher level of civilization — all technological developments will continue to accelerate and amplify our shortcomings, such as our self-centered focus on acquisition of material goods. Destructive social and ecological behavior will continue, through scarcity and abundance, as long as our human values are out of balance...

To which Jon Roland responds:

> ...The trouble with "spiritual values," is that they are a disease that is not very contagious. Despite high levels of exposure, too many people seem to be immune — enough to ruin things for everyone. It is not enough for people to be gentle and loving; most people are. They must also be farsighted, analytical, and vigorously active. And they must be prepared to be brutal in order to be kind. We can see how most of the leading lights in the environmental move-ment are too nice to bring themselves to do the kinds of things their understanding tells them must be done...

I think that both of these positions are legitimate — to a point. While it is true that a more mature spiritual orientation could save us, it is equally true that such an evolution would have to move at a pace far faster than plausible to be of any use to us at this point in time. And while it is true that some "vigorously active" decisions could also save us, it is equally true that any response "vigorous" enough to do any good in the time we have left would necessitate a totalitarian world government to implement it. While there's more than enough totalitarianism to go around, none of it is organized on that scale. Yet.

To ignore the obvious the way we have, intimates that our failure is one of incapacity rather than willed choice. In nature it is tests like these that determine the survival or extinction of a species. I personally don't see either of the above scenarios taking place — though the latter will probably materialize after it's too late to make much difference.

The future must inevitably be shaped by our collective indecisive muddling until we are caught up in the whirlpool of consequences created by at least six decades of ill-considered choices. When those consequences become everyday realities, too painful to ignore, our species will be forced to make some sudden and drastic adaptations. Only one thing seems certain: whatever the outcome, it will test everybody's capacity for survival.

Index

YOU WILL ALSO WANT TO READ:

☐ **14116 BUILDING WITH JUNK And Other Good Stuff,** *by Jim Broadstreet.* A complete guide to building and remodeling using recycled materials. This book shows how to find, store and use this good stuff. Covers floors, ceilings, walls, foundations, roofs, plumbing, wiring, utilities, windows, doors, and more including solar power. *1990, 8½ x 11, 159 pp, illustrated, hard cover. $19.95*

☐ **17054 HOW TO BUY LAND CHEAP, 4th Edition,** *by Edward Preston.* The author shows you how to buy good land all over the country for not much more than the $25 he payed for 8 lots. The book takes you through a step-by-step process. *1991, 5½ x 8½, 146 pp, illustrated, soft cover. $14.95*

☐ **17040 SHELTERS, SHACKS AND SHANTIES,** *by D.C. Beard.* A fascinating book with over 300 pen and ink illustrations and step-by-step instructions for building various types of shelters. One of the great classics of outdoor lore. *1914, 5 x 7, 259 pp, illustrated, soft cover. $12.95*

☐ **94105 SELECTIONS FROM FREE AMERICA,** *by Bolton Hall.* The 20 essays in this book cover subjects such as taxes, co-operative living, political reform, money reform, monopolies, free trade, and much more including an introduction by Mark Sullivan. *5½ x 8½, 199 pp, illustrated, soft cover. $8.95*

And much more! We offer the very finest in controversial and unusual books — please turn to our catalog announcement on the next page.

HHH2

LOOMPANICS UNLIMITED

PO Box 1197/Port Townsend, WA 98368

Please send me the titles I have checked above. I have enclosed $_____ (including $4.00 for shipping and handling of one to 3 titles, $6.00 for 4 or more).

Name _____

Address _____

City/State/Zip _____

Washington residents please include 7.8% sales tax.